The Complete Guide to JOB SHARING

PATRICIA LEE

with an Introduction by
Donald C. Lum,
Executive Vice President, Pfizer International

WALKER AND COMPANY  **NEW YORK**

Because job-sharing situations change with the changing needs of employees and employers, some names of individuals and companies have been changed.

First published in the United States of America
in 1983 by the Walker Publishing Company, Inc.

Published simultaneously in Canada by John Wiley & Sons
Canada, Limited, Rexdale, Ontario.

ISBN: 0-8027-0740-8 (hardcover)
          0-8027-7213-7 (paperback)
Library of Congress Catalog Card Number: 83-6470

Printed in the United States of America
10 9 8 7 6 5 4 3 2 1

Library of Congress Cataloging in Publication Data

Lee, Patricia.
   The complete guide to job sharing.

   Bibliography: p.
   Includes index.
   1. Job sharing. I. Title.
HD5110.15.L43 1983   331.25'72   83-6470
ISBN 0-8027-0740-8
ISBN 0-8027-7213-7 (pbk.)

IN MEMORY OF
Joanne Riggio,
friend and partner

Acknowledgments

Certainly, writing *The Complete Guide to Job Sharing* was, in itself, a shared job. Every author should have the pleasure of working with an editor like Ruth Cavin. Ruth's understanding, advice and encouragement helped me immeasurably in producing what I hope will be the key to all who seek to create shared jobs.

Many of my friends and colleagues assisted, through their support and suggestions, in this project. Special thanks are due

to Rene Brandeis, for sparking my interest in the need for greater opportunity to work less than full time;

to the staff of New Ways to Work and the members of the National Job Sharing Network, for their continuing support and sharing;

to Barbara Jacobson, for her researching and reference assistance;

to Nancy Quinn, for her wonderful typing job and for her enthusiasm; and

to my mother, Mary Bullock, for her constant support, and, most of all, for teaching me to share.

Patricia Lee
New York, 1983

Contents

Sample Forms and Models

Introduction:
Two Heads Are Better
Than One

Experience, not theory, has convinced me that two heads are indeed better than one. For the past two years, the administrative secretarial position that supports my function has been shared very successfully by former full-time employees who, for a variety of reasons, now prefer part-time work. And experience, not theory, is what this book is all about. Patricia Lee, who has assisted our company and others in installing job sharing, has translated her experience into practical guidance for those who seek part-time employment through job-sharing arrangements.

Ms. Lee's experience and mine, however, are only part of the story. The most important element may be the experience of individual job sharers for whom such arrangements open significant new opportunities. Job sharers at my company have offered the following comments on their experience:

> Job sharing has opened up a new and fulfilling future for me in terms of my career goals and simultaneously accomplishing what I consider another goal in life, raising my child. Many women such as myself, for reasons of income and personal fulfillment, find it necessary to have employment. Through job sharing I have "the best of both worlds."

1

I feel I am a better business person when I am job sharing, as my mental attitude is always positive and I report to my job feeling refreshed and enthusiastic. Through job sharing, I feel a sense of great accomplishment because I can handle both "jobs" (family and career) to my satisfaction as well as the satisfaction of the people involved in my life.

I feel that job sharing has given me a greater sense of achievement than I would be able to get from a traditional part-time job. I hope that in the future, there will be more job-sharing positions available for others who want to work part time in order to better balance home and career responsibilities or to pursue other interests.

Job sharing is a concept and practice whose time has come. Increasing numbers of people who want to work and need to work but who also have other responsibilities and occupations seek less than full-time employment. Traditionally, the number of part-time work opportunities was equivalent to the number of part-time jobs. A person seeking part-time employment had to locate an employer who defined some positions as part time. Job sharing is a significant breakthrough in that it allows employers to think in terms of full-time positions without thereby precluding part-time opportunities for employees. Job sharing is a form of part-time employment that does not require the creation of part-time jobs. Full-time jobs are shared by two or more (but usually two) people.

The increased interest in job sharing is not an isolated phenomenon. Job sharing is but one way to address a growing trend toward more flexible patterns of employment and work schedules. There have always been exceptions to the normal schedule—9:00 A.M. to 5:00 P.M., Monday to Friday, fifty-two weeks a year, with vacations increasing according to length of service. Some jobs had to be done on weekends, at night, or during certain seasons of the year. And in most cases, such departures from the prevailing work schedule have been viewed as less desirable.

Now, however, in a variety of circumstances, alternative work patterns and schedules are viewed as desirable and are sought out by increasing numbers of employees and job seekers. For example, where husband and wife are employed, one or both may desire and find financially feasible a reduced-work, reduced-pay arrangement. The objective may be to seek further education, devote time to child rearing, or pursue leisure interests. Similar objectives may lead an employee to seek a full-time but flexible-hours work schedule. Older employees who are nearing retirement may wish to reduce time on the job as a way of making a more gradual transition to retirement. Or retired persons with a need for supplemental income may seek part-time employment.

Whatever the motives, the interest in more flexible work arrangements appears to be growing. Enlightened employers know that among those seeking such alternatives to the usual pattern are numerous talented individuals. Job sharing is one way to assure access to that pool of talent.

But access to talented part-time job seekers is not the only motivation for the employer. Two heads, in many instances, are indeed better than one for several reasons. First, if properly matched, two incumbents are likely to bring a wider range of abilities and skills to a job than one person will. An able supervisor will take advantage of the abilities of each. Second, for some full-time employees, the ability to concentrate on the job is affected by the pull of nonwork responsibilities or interests. If financial circumstances allow such persons to move to a shared job, thus permitting greater attention to nonwork interests, improvement in productivity may result. More will probably be accomplished by such individuals in the two or three days a week of a shared job than in two or three days of a full-time five-day workweek. For most workers, particularly those in jobs entailing considerable discretion, there is a certain dilution of effort over a five-day period; a more productive concentration of effort seems to characterize the shorter workweek. Third, two heads are better than one in that tasks tend to move to completion more quickly. At least where participants in a shared secretarial, clerical, or administrative job are conscientious, they will complete many tasks before their shortened workweek ends rather than pass them on to their job partner or hold them unfinished until the following week.

Of course, such positive results are not guaranteed. Two heads will be better than one only if certain conditions are met. First, the job sharers must be compatible. At least this is the case where the job is not physically divisible into two distinct parts. Second, ability levels ought not to be significantly different, although different types of skills that complement one another may be desirable. Third, scheduling must be negotiated to meet the needs of all affected parties, including the supervisor and any other receivers of services, in addition to the jobholders. Fourth, particularly where the responsibilities of the job sharers overlap (as in a secretarial position, for example) good communication— not just good intentions or a good relationship, but a good communication *system*—is essential. This may be the most critical ingredient of all. Fifth, the incumbents must be conscientious and responsible, desirous of helping each other and meeting the objectives of the job as a team. If they regularly leave unfinished or undesirable tasks for the other party, the job-sharing effort is likely to fail.

It should be recognized, too, that job sharing is not for everyone, nor is it workable in all situations. And there can be disadvantages as well as advantages. As part-time employees, job sharers accumulate less experience within a given amount of time than full-time workers do. This factor, when combined with the fact that not all jobs lend themselves to job sharing, may mean that career advancement opportunities are more limited and slower in coming than for persons holding full-time jobs. In addition, job sharing is still seen as something of a novelty by most employers and may have associations similar to temporary employment. It may be assumed that such employees are less committed to the organization. One of the challenges to management is to overcome these perceptions so that job sharers are seen as permanent employees with the potential for long-term commitment and contribution to the organization. Appropriate career development opportunities must be made available.

On the basis of my own limited but positive experience with job sharing, and because it meets a valid employee need, I recommend it for consideration by employers generally. I believe job sharing is one of several ways that organizations can build more flexibility into the employment options they offer. Such flexibility helps meet a growing diversity of needs and interests on the part of employees. Guidance like that provided here by Ms. Lee can help assure that such arrangements are successful and to the benefit of employer and employee alike.

DONALD C. LUM, *Executive Vice President*
Pfizer International

1

"The Best of Both Worlds!"

Job sharers nationwide echo these words—and with good reason. Thousands of women and men are striving to pursue their careers, maintain their professional dignity, and spend *less than full time* doing it. Whether these individuals chose to work less than full time in order to raise a family, pursue an advanced education or a second career, or prepare for retirement, their ranks are swelling dramatically.

Job sharing, the innovative concept whereby two employees hold what was formerly one full-time position, is paving the way. Determined to utilize their education and training, these new pioneers have blazed a trail through the canyons of public- and private-sector organizations, confronting the corporate colossus to open a new frontier for permanent part-time employment.

Two employees, or even three, can determine with their employer how to restructure existing positions, share responsibilities, divide fringe benefits, and schedule time to meet personal needs and fulfill job requirements. Salary and fringe benefits are prorated.

As early as 1937, in a Carmel, California, cannery, Thomas Butman approached his employer with a proposal to share his job. He was turned down.

Not so now. Over the past few years, hundreds of workers,

6

on an individual basis or as part of a large employer program, have participated in this unique work arrangement.

The past forty years have witnessed sweeping changes in the American work force. Perhaps most significant is the increase in the number of working women, who today make up over 43 percent of our labor force. Of all mothers with children under the age of three, 42 percent work. Dual-career families and single heads of households receive increasing attention, from both the business and the social sectors.

In addition, it has been suggested that young people pursue prolonged education because there are no jobs and that advances in technology and business know-how demand recurrent education throughout life.

Good health and increased life expectancy have dispelled the myth of less productive older workers. The threat of runaway inflation alarms many, especially those restricted to living on a fixed income. For retirees and preretirement employees, that concern means prolonging their work life, preferably on a part-time basis.

Quality of life has become a major consideration of our society, and a good many things included in that catchphrase require more free time. Students, writers, artists, entrepreneurs, and in some cases, those who wish to pursue more than one career are all concerned with maintaining their jobs on a less than full-time basis.

In addition to responding to individual needs, job sharing offers an opportunity to stretch the job market during an economic downturn.

The positions of museum curators, parole officers, secretaries, lawyers, engineers, school administrators, career counselors, doctors, teachers, and librarians are just a few of the jobs now being shared. In some cases, tasks are assigned to each sharer; in others, the effort is collaborative.

Take, for example, the senior personnel representative at a

major aerospace technology corporation. Five years ago, Lynn was a personnel assistant in industrial relations, and Janice was a personnel representative reporting to the compensation and staffing supervisor. When Lynn became pregnant and Janice and her husband were planning their family, the two women explored the concept of job sharing. Management initially turned down their proposal as unworkable but ultimately agreed to give it a try. At first, the tasks of personnel representative in the employment section were divided, with Lynn handling nonexempt clerical openings and Janice in charge of technical and administrative exempt recruiting. After convincing their employer that this split was unrealistic, they are now recognized by management as a team handling all openings. Their job is shared on a collaborative basis. (*Note:* As of this writing, both women have left this position, one to return to full-time work and one to another less than full-time position. They have been replaced by a second generation of job sharers.)

On the other hand, when Lisa and Marilyn shared the position of science/feature writer at a major New York teaching hospital, they did so by dividing tasks. Lisa's specialty was writing about scientific, research-oriented subjects; she was also responsible for a monthly in-house publication. Marilyn's emphasis was on administrative and family care issues, and she handled a semi-annual brochure distributed to the general public. Press releases were written by both writers, with Lisa handling the scientific material, Marilyn the general-information releases. When the need arose, Lisa and Marilyn collaborated on assignments most successfully. Once, when Lisa was bedridden with a serious illness, Marilyn sat at a typewriter next to Lisa's bed, and Lisa dictated the article. The publication met its deadline.

Job sharing offers a potpourri of time-schedule possibilities. Generally, there is a fifty-fifty split; but it can be sixty-forty, or, as happened at one major university when a position became more complex, the shared time was expanded to 75 percent and 66 percent (141 percent) of a normal workweek. Scheduling can range from half days to every six months and all points in between.

One woman who shares two jobs spends half of every day as a librarian and the other half as a student counselor—and she thrives on the variety.

The directors of career counseling at one New York college split that job into two and a half days apiece, with one sharer working Monday morning, Wednesday, and Friday and the other working Monday afternoon, Tuesday, and Thursday. They have lunch together every Monday to review the week's happenings.

In Wisconsin, a parole officer works six months straight and spends the other six months developing a real estate business. His partner uses her free six months to enjoy time with her family.

An unusual, successful job-sharing program has been developed at a large insurance company, where 240 employees share 120 positions. Their schedule is one week on, one week off.

There's no limit to the ways a schedule can be developed.

Just as there is tremendous flexibility in time scheduling, so salaries, benefits, space, and tasks can be shared in a variety of ways.

In many cases, the salary is prorated on the basis of the time spent at the job (usually fifty-fifty); but in some cases, when the skills of the partners are unequal, the salary levels reflect that inequality. The members of one job-sharing team of secretaries were at different grade levels; one partner has been the incumbent in the job, while the other came from a different department at a lower salary grade. For their first year of sharing, their salary rates were different because one partner was in training. As her skills and experience were brought up to match those of the incumbent, her salary was increased.

Most job-sharing teams share the same space, but sometimes, where larger areas are available, each sharer has his or her own desk or even office.

As described later on, benefits can also be shared in a wide variety of ways. Usually, the type of benefits and the way they are shared are at the discretion of the employer.

Law firms have been job sharing for decades. Although each attorney essentially works full time, the partnership structure allows for job-sharing opportunities constantly. Corporate attorneys utilize the talents of a litigating partner for an antitrust case; a labor attorney refers a tax problem to the firm's tax department; another partner covers a case load while the assigned attorney is in court, on vacation, or ill. The concept is the same: *a team at work.*

Employers are discovering that job sharing has a positive effect on both the worker and the workplace. Some of the pluses cited by enthusiastic employers of job-sharing teams are

increased productivity

the opportunity to recruit from a broader labor pool

retention of valued employees

reduced turnover

greater flexibility in work scheduling

a wider range of skills in one job title

new options for older employees

more energy on the job

reduction of absenteeism

continuity of job performance

Job sharing also offers the option of creating part-time professional employment without rewriting the organization chart.

"There's no question that I get 200 percent from my writers.

It is a unique interplay of two people, two brains, two different writing styles that work to perfection.'' That's what Courtney Harmes, director of public affairs, had to say about Lisa and Marilyn, the sharers of the hospital science/feature writer position.

What makes someone decide to share a job? Risk becoming an innovator? Challenge the status quo?

Job sharers are people concerned with optimum use of time. For many, job sharing means raising a family while maintaining a career; for others, it can open the door to second or even dual careers. For retirees, job sharing may solve growing economic and social problems while providing the opportunity to maintain the dignity of a professional position and explore other interests or participate in volunteer activities.

Many women find that the biological clock makes the decision for them. A few years ago, women put off childbearing until they were established in their careers, most waiting until their late thirties. Now, younger, career-oriented women are pressing for ways to blend professional life with family life.

DUAL-CAREER FAMILIES

Confronted with the choice between professional achievement and the rewards of parenting, women are still forced to decide whether they will place the family first or choose challenging careers, forgoing motherhood. For more and more men, the role of nurturer is replacing the allure of being a "company man." Dual-career families are placed under tremendous stress in an effort to combine professionalism and parenthood.

Superwoman or Supermom

For Elaine and John, their fifteenth wedding anniversary marked a milestone. Time was running out, if they intended to have a family, it would have to be soon.

Elaine was reluctant to give up her position as director of career counseling at a prestigious New York college. On the other hand, she had seen too many of her friends fall into the Superwoman trap. That was definitely not for her. John, supportive of Elaine's career goals, encouraged her to seek alternatives and remain in her profession.

Determined to find a successful formula for blending career and family, Elaine explored various possibilities. With the aid of her intern/assistant, Barbara, she researched possible avenues to achieving the perfect mix. Their research turned up job sharing as the most viable solution. Barbara would be the perfect person for Elaine to share the position with; she was well known on campus and had a proven track record with the college administration.

Armed with their well-researched proposal, Elaine and Barbara met with the vice president of student affairs. Reluctant at first, the vice president finally agreed—with one hitch—Elaine and Barbara would share the job, but ultimate responsibility would rest with Elaine, the incumbent.

Disappointed but not disheartened, Elaine and Barbara set out, determined to prove just how well job sharing would work. Now, their vice president is an enthusiastic supporter. Admittedly not a risk taker, she firmly states that she would be willing to take on another team of job sharers now, even newcomers to the organization!

The Case for One Caseload, Two Doctors

Dr. O'Malley is a full-time anesthesiologist at Mercy Medical Center in New City, California. Some people find "Dr. O'Malley" a little confusing. Two days of the week, Dr. Jane O'Malley is on duty; and the other three days, the job belongs to Dr. Eileen O'Malley.

Drs. O'Malley are sisters, and they divide one permanent full-time position at the hospital. In addition, they share seven children. Each is married and the mother of three and four children, respectively. Sharing their professional and parental responsibilities came naturally. "I'm her other half and vice versa," Eileen O'Malley explains about her sister, Jane. "We've found it's a reasonable way to keep your hand in the profession and have time for a family. It's given us the best of both worlds!"

The Washington Bureau Desk

Jack Harley's promotion to the Washington Bureau of the *Kansas City Daily Sun* should have been a cause for celebration. It wasn't.

Jack and his wife, Molly, were both reporters for the *Sun*. Raising their three young children while maintaining professional careers was not much of a problem as long as they were close to both sets of grandparents in Kansas City.

The move to Washington would be a personal and professional crisis. It would cause a major upheaval in their family life. Either Molly would have to give up her profession, or they would have to turn their children over to strangers in a strange city while she worked.

The Harleys did a lot of brainstorming and came up with a proposal for the newspaper: Let them share the job. The *Sun* bought the idea, and while heads turn now and then at the Washington Bureau to see who's at the desk, the coverage is always top drawer.

By no means, though, is job sharing just a family affair! The average worker's goal of a chicken in every pot has been replaced by considerations of quality of life, life planning, and more recently, back to basics.

Reeducation and changing careers are other needs that job sharing serves. It's no longer necessary to take a long, expensive sabbatical in order to pursue a degree or walk two roads. The job sharer remains in one career while exploring other opportunities.

NEW OR CHANGING CAREERS

Finding the right job is almost always difficult; without experience, it's impossible. Reentering the job market or changing careers can mean years of entry-level jobs before achieving parity with your peers.

240 Share 120

At one major life insurance company, there are many women who have reentered the job market through shared jobs. When Marie DeMaio's youngest went off to college, she suddenly felt closed in at home; but after spending thirty-three years as a housewife, she was too frightened to take a full-time job. Marie's fears were not groundless. Many women confronted with the "empty nest" syndrome are fearful of making a commitment to a totally different life-style in unfamiliar surroundings.

Margie Welsh had too much time on her hands. She didn't want a job that would keep her from visits with friends and family; she enjoyed the luxury of shopping in uncrowded stores, playing in the afternoon with grandchildren, and having a friendly bridge game now and then. But she couldn't do that all the time.

Both these women found the answer through the insurance company's job-sharing program, where for the past several years 240 people have shared 120 clerical jobs. Each works a schedule of one week on, one week off.

Turning Points

The twentieth reunion of the class of '56 at Smith College was a turning point for Carole Bruno. Happily married to a successful attorney, with two growing children, Carole had worked most of her married life. Looking around at her classmates, Carole recognized a real need—a need for direction and personal satisfaction not only for herself but also for the other women she saw there, who were seeking outside fulfillment now that their children were grown.

Carole wanted to do more than work; she wanted to do something personally meaningful. She also wanted to aid these and other women seeking direction in their lives. She knew that for her generation, women's lib had often produced more conflicts than answers.

Carole's first step was to go back to school for her master's degree in career development. During that period, she zeroed in on the best schools offering programs not only for young women entering the work force but also for older women reentering the job market.

It was during her internship at such a college that Carole met Nancy Herman. Nancy and Carole worked well together, and when Nancy confided that she and her husband, Mark, wanted to start a family and she wanted to cut back on her work time, the two women focused on job sharing as the means for both to achieve their personal goals. The college would still be provided with the best possible career counseling services.

Carole was able to realize a long-term dream when she and two colleagues opened their own career counseling consulting firm. Her position at the college provides her with the professional stature necessary for recognition in her field, and the diversity provided by her private practice and academic work satisfy her personal need for broad horizons.

WALKING TWO ROADS

The ability to develop creative talents, market free-lance skills, or start a new business usually hinges on having a sizable nest egg, one that is adequate to support oneself and sometimes one's family over the incomeless period before the idea takes hold.

Creative Freedom and Job Security

Lisa Morrow was sick and tired of banging out copy five days a week, fifty weeks a year, year after year—and Lisa was successful! Successful at copywriting, yes, but not successful at finding time to do what she really wanted to do: write fiction. By the time she finished her forty or more hours a week at a major New York public relations firm, she was mentally and physically exhausted. A short story here and there was about all she had time for.

She had to do something. What? She couldn't afford to quit working, but she could afford to change jobs. Lisa answered an ad for a "Part-time writer, two days," and out of over 200 applicants, she got the job as science/feature writer in the public affairs department of a hospital.

What Lisa didn't know when she applied for the job was that she would be sharing it. Lisa had a counterpart, Marilyn Greene, who worked three days a week at the same job.

For Marilyn, who is divorced and the mother of two teenage children, the shared job gives her time to be both Mommy and a salaried professional and still allows her to do free-lance writing. She now can claim co-authorship of four successful novels. Not a bad arrangement!

One Head, Two Hats

Six months of the year, Tom Green is a parole officer; the other six months, Tom is a successful real estate agent.

How does he do it? Simple—he shares his job with Mary Lowell, who spends *her* free time with her family.

Tom had often explored the possibility of selling real estate, but the uncertainty of immediate income to support his family made those explorations a mere exercise in futility. Tom just couldn't afford to take the risks inherent in entering a new field where income is based primarily on commissions; he had his wife and two small children to consider. And he liked his work as a parole officer; he just didn't like doing it all the time.

Tom and Mary were both full-time parole officers when the state launched its job-sharing program, the original objective of which was to define and study 50 shared positions in state service. This goal was surpassed; 110 half-time positions were eventually put in place and later evaluated. Tom and Mary were among those state employees who expressed a desire to participate in the program. Their request was somewhat unique in that they each wanted to work full time six months of the year and have no continuing responsibilities in the months they didn't work. They asked to share one case load; both felt this was the most practical job-sharing arrangement because a parole officer must be on call twenty-four hours a day.

Implementation of Tom and Mary's job sharing went smoothly. Their supervisor did not have to consider scheduling, office coverage, training, or hiring procedures. The main concern was to prevent a disruption of client services during the transition time. This, too, was worked out; and with a one-week overlap, service was maintained and clients felt no anxiety or difficulty about having two parole officers.

A NOTE TO TEACHERS

From nursery school to university, more and more teachers are "teaming up," to the benefit of student and teacher alike.

For one pair of high school English teachers, the sharing extends beyond the classroom. Joan Dawson and Mary Hughes have responsibility for one full-time position. They not only teach the standard classes, but also fulfill study hall, supervisory and extra-help duties. While Joan teaches during the morning hours Mary takes care of her own child and Joan's as well, in the afternoon they switch places.

In another part of the country, third graders are benefiting from what one class member terms a "neat" arrangement. Their teachers split the week, with one partner working Monday, Tuesday and Wednesday morning and the other partner taking over Wednesday afternoon, Thursday and Friday. One third grader insists, "I learn faster than with just one teacher. That gets kind of boring." The teachers believe that sharing the job is a way to avoid teacher burnout. "If you do have a difficult child and are ready to burn out, you're relieved of the strain and conflict. Also, if a child has a problem, it's supportive to have two teachers with the same viewpoint when we speak with the parents."

Teachers aren't the only ones touting the benefits of job sharing. Many administrators feel that job sharing teachers are fresher on the job and in a better frame of mind. "The time spent in class is effective, and it's time in which they're giving 100 percent."

For teachers who do decide to share, there are some special considerations beyond the economics and egonomics of job sharing. It's important that both teachers have the same educational philosophy. As with any job-sharing arrangements, scheduling must be designed to meet the needs of the sharers and in this case, the curriculum and the students. Responsibilities can be split or shared. In some cases, one teacher may feel stronger in math and reading while the other may shine in the social sciences. In other cases, both teachers teach all the subjects. It must also be determined how the noncurricular responsibilities will be handled. Will both teachers be required to attend some activities? Can only one attend, representing the team? Working with your administrator you should decide ahead of time how you will handle faculty meetings, parent conferences, committee assignments, club sponsorships, open house, field trips, PTA meetings, school picnics and parties, yard and bus duty.

Communications are also essential. Class plans should be prepared jointly. Determine how you will cover the myriad of details that a teacher needs to keep track of.

Yet another area where the teaching team must take special

precautions is in substitution. Are you prepared to substitute for each other in case of illness? Can emergency baby-sitters be called on if one teacher needs to go back on a full-time basis for a while?

Most parents have had favorable reactions to teachers job sharing. It is, however, essential that the job-sharing arrangement be explained in advance, in order to avoid confusion. Will both of you attend parent-teacher conferences? Will you split the student body so that one teacher confers with certain parents and the partner confers with others?

Finally, you should decide in advance how you will handle reversibility. What if one or both of you want to go back to full time? Should you include this contingency in your job-sharing proposal? Certainly, the possibility exists that at some future date you will want to return to full time. It would be wise for you and your partner to make this decision in advance and perhaps establish a review period at the end of which time reversibility can be determined.

SENIORS

Another group for whom job sharing is moving to the forefront is senior citizens. From the worker's point of view, it can mean "getting the gold watch *and* keeping the job." Employers can keep skilled workers on the job while providing training for younger workers moving up.

Early retirement as a status symbol is beginning to tarnish. The soaring cost of living, a desire to remain productive, and improved health are reversing the trend toward retirement at age 60. Experts are predicting that by the mid-1980s early retirement will be on the way out. Research indicates that older persons want to work, but not full time. Of the present population who continue working after 65, 69 percent are working part time voluntarily.

Most major employers are looking at ways to keep their

skilled older workers on the job. Because the population is aging, the percentage of retirees is increasing at a faster pace than the percentage of active workers. Soon there will be a premium on younger workers, and employers will recognize the wisdom of employing older workers.

To retain its skilled older employees, industry is experimenting with alternative work patterns that include flexible schedules, part-time work, and other changes intended to adapt the job to the special needs of older workers. Chapter 4 explores in depth what employers are doing to accommodate the needs of their older workers.

Since the turn of the century, workers have lessened their standard workweek from sixty or more hours to the now widely accepted forty-hour week. The number of people working fewer than thirty-four hours a week has increased over the past twenty years from 14 to 33 percent. Longer vacations, sabbaticals, and holidays have also taken the spotlight. It all spells *time!*

Time to enjoy the good life! Art, music, family, friends, relaxing, and recharging the battery all require more leisure time, and workers are willing to make the trade: time for money.

What are the basic requirements for job sharing? What jobs can be shared? Who can share?

Basically, most jobs can be shared. Careful exploration of the tasks involved, of time requirements, of any special logistics, and sound planning are needed. However, there are two very important things to determine before approaching the planning of sharing a job: the *economics* and *egonomics*.

THE ECONOMICS

Make sure you can afford it! It's important to budget for half a salary. Your reason for job sharing may be to pursue a second career or open a new business. Until these new endeavors are firmly established, *don't* count on them adding to your new net income.

Following is a sample job sharer's budget work sheet. You may come up with other items to add under living expenses—education, pension plans, investment portfolios, and so on. Be sure to cover *all* your expenses.

In computing your new net income, be sure to take into consideration the reduced rate of taxation. If your present weekly gross salary is $300.00 and you are married, claiming two dependents, your net income (in New York City) is $223.55. If you share your job fifty-fifty, your new gross salary will be $150.00; however, your new net income will be $123.77, not $111.73, reflecting the reduced rate of taxation.

Other items that will be affected are child care, commutation, and dry cleaning bills. Don't forget that you may now have to pay one-half of your medical insurance, so that expense will increase.

By using a *running balance,* you can catch the red lights in your expenses and determine what (if anything) can be eliminated.

THE EGONOMICS

Equally important in considering a shared job is the "egonomics." Measuring your feelings is every bit as important as measuring your money. Not everyone is cut out to share their niche in the workplace, and it's important to determine if you're one of the people who are not. Job sharing can be a lot like Cinderella's slipper—you could wind up with nothing more than blisters. If you have at one time or another exchanged business cards, chest swelling with pride at the grand title appearing beneath your name, are you ready to see two names above that title? Two names on the office door? Two sets of pens and pencils in the desk drawer? Somebody else using *your* typewriter? If you answered no to any of these questions, stop right here. Job sharing isn't for you.

EMPLOYEE'S MONTHLY BUDGET WORK SHEET

	Present Monthly Gross Income	Adjusted Monthly Gross Income
	$ *2,000.00*	$ *1,000.00*
Federal, state & local taxes (single person claiming 2 deductions)	- *738.57*	- *251.16*
	Present Net Income	Adjusted Net Income
	$ *1,261.43*	$ *748.84*

MONTHLY LIVING EXPENSES

Item	Amount	Running Balance*	
Housing	$ *320.00*	$ *941.43*	$ *428.84*
Transportation	*50.00*	*891.43*	*378.84*
Insurance	*70.00*	*821.43*	*308.84*
Food	*150.00*	*671.43*	*158.84*
Clothing	*60.00*	*611.43*	*98.84*
Medical/dental	*20.00*	*591.43*	*78.84*
Savings	*200.00*	*391.43*	*-121.16*
Vacation	*150.00*	*241.43*	*-271.16*
Entertainment	*100.00*	*141.43*	*-371.16*
Mad money	*50.00*	*91.43*	*-421.16*
THE BOTTOM LINE	$ *1,170*	$ *91.43*	$ *-421.16*

*If halfway through the running balance you come up with $0 in adjusted net income, list those items where you can positively cut back:

Savings, vacation, entertainment, mad money

It is important to determine if your job title is a major component of your self-image. Would you continue to feel like a professional if you were on the job less than full time? Do you worry about the ball being dropped if you're not there in person to see that the job gets gone? Do you really enjoy your vacation time? Are you organized? If you are taken ill, are the components of your job organized in such a way that a few telephone calls can ensure smooth operations until you return to work? Do you prefer brainstorming to tackling a problem on your own? Have you ever been a member of a task force? Did you enjoy the experience? Are you willing to teach others your job so that you can move on to other areas? Do your co-workers, supervisors, and subordinates feel comfortable about including you in team projects? Are you willing to accept 50 percent of the accolades for a job well done and 50 percent of the blame if something goes wrong? Are you a communicator? Do you enjoy open, clear exchanges of information? Do you enjoy collaboration and cooperation? Are team projects fun? Are you willing to take risks and be the forerunner with new ideas? Do you take new ideas and map out methods of achievement and patiently see the project through? Are your office and/or desk and equipment "sacred ground"? Are you rankled if someone else uses your space? Is having the boss's ear essential to your sense of security? Do you resent getting instructions secondhand? Do you need constant pats on the back to keep you going? Would you enjoy sharing a problem with a peer? Would another head improve your job performance?

Some people really do prefer working alone, and that's just fine—but it's not fine for job sharing. You will need to be part of a team, and for that spirit of teamwork, you should enjoy working with a partner and feel comfortable trusting that partner to hold up his or her half of the job. Otherwise, you will wind up feeling not only the burden of a full-time job but also the concern about an additional person's performance.

* * *

This book provides the tools for employers to create job-sharing programs for employees seeking to share their existing jobs and for individuals who want to apply for employment on a job-shared basis.

For individuals, it is still easier to share one's existing job than to apply for a shared job. Quite simply, once you are in a job, you are a known entity. Employers who might otherwise be reluctant to experiment with a new work design will take more risks with a valued employee than with a stranger.

It is not impossible to apply for a job on a shared basis; it has been done quite successfully. However, you may find that it is still a harder row to hoe.

2

Sharing the Job
You Now Have

As stated earlier, you have a better chance of finding a shared job by restructuring your present position so that it can be shared than by setting out, with or without a partner, to find a job for two. Both methods bring results, but one is more productive than the other. So if you are working now, look hard at what you are doing and at the policies of your company, and evaluate the situation in terms of that restructuring.

Some of the things that have to be done apply equally to both situations: finding a partner and deciding what each of you have to contribute, deciding how you will divide your time, agreeing on how you will allot whatever fringe benefits are available, and creating ways to keep the lines of communication flowing accurately and efficiently both between the two of you and with a supervisor. Other tasks are specific to applying for a new job, and these will be dealt with in a separate chapter.

Before embarking on the conversion of your job from a single-person job to a shared one, it is essential that you determine if, in fact, you really want to maintain this position on a less than full-time basis. You must analyze your motivation for and commitment to sharing your job, your supervisor's attitudes toward change, the organization's willingness to accept change, and the possible problems you will encounter.

The first step is to take a look at your present job.

YOU, YOUR JOB, AND YOUR WORK ENVIRONMENT

You and Your Job

Is this the job you want to stay in? Is this job important enough to you that you are willing to devote the extra time and energy required to redesigning it? Do you have the tenacity to see the program through and sell it to your employer? Commitment and pride in your job are absolutely essential if you are going to accomplish your goal.

Establish a realistic time schedule for yourself, and stay with it. The conversion of your job could take anywhere from one to six months; make sure you're willing to stick it out. You should also determine some limits: If you are not allowed to share your job, will you quit?

Recognize that in initiating this change, the principal burden of responsibility falls on your shoulders. It is up to you to determine how the job you want can be shared, where to find a partner, what the cost (and benefits) to your employer will be, and how your time and your partner's time will be scheduled. Be prepared to devote a great deal of time to the research and preparation of your proposal.

Your Value to the Organization

Fundamental to the success of restructuring your job is your value as an employee. If you've been on the job only three months, it is rather unlikely that your new employer is going to be willing to institute a program just to suit your needs. Be sure that you play a vital role in your organization and that you have a proven track record to point to when presenting your case. This is a good time to examine your strengths and accomplishments, assess your job performance, demonstrated talents and abilities.

Make a list of improvements you have instituted, special programs you have created, supervisory skills you have demonstrated, special talents you have brought to the job, and any suggestions that management has utilized. All these strengthen your negotiating position.

Next, explore your work environment. Your supervisor, organization management, personnel department, and co-workers are all keys to your success.

Your Supervisor

Is your supervisor an innovator, responding to new ideas positively, willing to experiment with new ways to do things? Or will he or she balk at changing the system? The support of your supervisor will be essential to your success. What is your relationship? Are you able to discuss problems openly? Do you and your supervisor share ideas, brainstorm? Does your supervisor rely on you to handle your job, cope with responsibility, and come through in a crunch? Are you an important, contributing member of the team? Would your absence create a gap in performance?

Will your supervisor go to bat with management for your proposal? The support and cooperation of your supervisor is basic in preparing your job-sharing proposal and in seeking a partner. Your supervisor may even know of potential partners within the department or organization.

Conversely, if your supervisor's reaction to your sharing your job is negative, beware! It may lead to insurmountable roadblocks in your path. This should be a positive experience for both of you. Getting your job-sharing proposal accepted by management won't mean a thing if the first week it is in operation you are hit from left field by an unhappy supervisor. Make your supervisor your aide and adviser while you are researching your proposal, and you will strengthen your support system.

Part of restructuring your job will include decisions on how and what you want to negotiate for when discussing the proposal with your employer.

Co-Workers

Identify all the players, anyone who will be directly involved in the final discussions and decision about restructuring your job. Look to see where support and resistence lie so that you can chart your course more carefully. It's human nature for anyone to ask, "What's in it for me?" so when you're discussing your job-sharing proposal, keep in mind what co-workers stand to gain and to lose. Do they have any problems that would be eased or solved by your sharing your job? On the other hand, would you be creating new problems?

Who are the innovators in your organization, and can you discuss job sharing with them? If their initial reaction is negative, try to find out why. Has the program been tried before? Where? By whom? For how long? See if you can talk with the people who were involved in the program so that you can avoid the snags they came up against. Other programs within the company may also provide a source of a future partner.

Organization Management

More and more organizations are concerned with progressive management of human resources. Research is constantly under way to assess employee attitudes, improve productivity, enhance employee skills, and develop new, more effective recruiting techniques. Try to find out if the organization you are approaching considers itself people-oriented, progressive, in the vanguard of human resources management. Are there any flexible work pattern programs currently in active use, such as flextime, part-time employment, and sabbaticals? Are these programs successful? If so, why are they successful? If not, why not? Does management point to these foresighted programs with pride? If so, you're in luck. It is likely to mean that there are innovators at the top, open to exploring new ideas.

The Personnel Department

Most organizations have formal personnel policy manuals that are available to all employees. You should have one. If such a manual is not available, you should ask someone in the personnel department about the following policies:

> Are permanent part-time personnel restricted through the use of department head counts? That is, is each individual employee listed as a full-time slot? This system makes it difficult to sell sharing a job because it will increase the head count.
>
> Are permanent part-time employees included in the company's fringe benefits package? This varies from organization to organization, with some companies providing full coverage for part-time employees, others prorating benefits according to time worked, and still others limiting enrollment to employees who work over twenty-five or thirty hours a week.

Other areas that should be discussed with your personnel department are retirement benefits, union contracts, and payroll management (the difference between manual and computer-prepared payrolls will affect the cost to your employer of having two employees sharing the job). Part of restructuring your job will include decisions on how and what you want to negotiate for when discussing the proposal with your employer.

PREPARING AND PRESENTING
YOUR PROPOSAL TO YOUR EMPLOYER

When you present your proposal to your employer, it should contain the following components, which will be described in detail in later chapters:

An up-to-date description of your present job.

An outline of your skills and your partner's and how they correspond to the job description.

A breakdown of how the job responsibilities, major and minor, will be divided.

A work-time schedule stating its advantages for the company, peak-time coverage, vacation coverage, holidays, reduced absenteeism, and so on. It may be wise to present alternatives if more than one type of schedule is feasible for the two of you.

A suggested division of fringe benefits and what their costs will be.

The communication tools you and your partner will utilize.

How you plan to communicate with your supervisor.

How your job sharing will affect the rest of the organization, including co-workers and unions, and any possible public relations benefits.

Backup information on job sharing—history, others utilizing the concept, and the like.

When you prepare your proposal, keep in mind that well-written, well-organized documents are easy to read and are more likely to be read. It is suggested that you include an over-all summary of your proposal, describing very briefly what each section covers. If possible use some sort of binder with tabs indicating where each section starts. It would be best if you could present your written proposal to your employer a day (no more) in advance of your meeting. He or she will need a chance to become familiar with the information, but you'll want to submit it close enough to the meeting for the information still to be fresh in your employer's mind.

When you approach an employer, you should anticipate questions as much as possible and have your answers ready. However, should a question arise for which you do not have a ready response, you can offer to do additional research. After all, even Einstein didn't have all the answers.

It would certainly be worthwhile, if you and your partner can, to "role play" this meeting with a friend or colleague who can discuss the job from an objective point of view. This will help you to be more at ease when faced with the actual discussion. If you have any doubts about the strength of your proposal, don't hesitate to contact one of the organizations listed in the appendixes of this book. Your role playing and/or contact with a support organization will show up any weak links or perhaps prove that there aren't any, that you've done a really splendid job of preparation. In either case, that extra boost will add to your confidence when you make your presentation.

Your commitment to job sharing, your thorough research, your past experience, and your position as a valued employee should convince your employer that this is a program worth pursuing, and chances are good that he or she will work with you in resolving any minor unanswered questions.

You are now ready to move on to the mechanics of sharing your job.

YOUR JOB DESCRIPTION

Well-written, up-to-date job descriptions are vital tools in effective human resources management. You were probably shown a
copy of your job description when you were hired. It may even
have been recently updated. If, however, you do not have a job
description, or if, perhaps, you feel the one you have is somewhat
out-of-date, this is the time to write one. In order to restructure
your job, you will need the framework and guidelines provided by
a well-written, currently valid outline of what you do.

What a Job Description Does

Job descriptions serve many functions. Before attempting to write
one, it would be well to understand just what those functions are
and how they apply to you.

> Job descriptions, when used in conjunction with organiza-
> tion charts and functional statements, identify the work to be
> performed in particular jobs and the interrelationships of
> these jobs with others in the organization.

> An accurate job description is vital in giving recruiting and
> screening personnel a clear picture of what a job is all about.

> In hiring and placement, the personnel department must rely
> on the job description for specifications concerning knowl-
> edge, responsibility, and physical working requirements.
> According to government regulations, preemployment tests
> must be strictly in line with job requirements.

> Most employers will allow a prospective employee or one
> newly hired to examine the job description to give him or
> her a more complete picture of what will be expected and the
> person will be able to measure how that picture compares
> with his or her self-image, expectations, and aspirations.

Training and development is another area where up-to-date job descriptions provide important planning tools by identifying the education, experience, and skills required for performance.

Job descriptions also allow personnel planners to focus on relationships among jobs and spot the places where the education, experience, and skills acquired in one job can lead to the next rung on the career ladder.

Wage and salary administrators utilize job descriptions for job evaluation, grading, classification, compensation surveys, pay structures, and standards of performance.

The Parts of a Job Description

Job Identification: This includes the job title, status (exempt or nonexempt), the date it was written and revised, department and location, the title of the immediate supervisor, the person who prepared the job description and who it was approved by, and the signature of the preparer and approver.

Job Summary: This section gives a brief description of the job, highlighting the job's general characteristics. In a few carefully selected words, it presents clearly and succinctly what the jobholder must do on his or her job.

Job Duties: This section states major activities that must be performed in carrying out the job. That is, it lists major duties and responsibilities but not necessarily the tasks required for their performance. Measures of performance can be applied to these duty statements and can be used as a basis for setting the primary goals of the job. This section represents an outline and is not meant to be all-inclusive; rather, it describes the duties related to the job's major performance requirements. Each major duty or responsibility may be described in one sentence.

Accountabilities: This is a brief description of the major results achieved when the job duties are satisfactorily performed. This section serves as a guide in setting performance goals and standards and is useful as a reference in preparing performance appraisals.

Job Specifications: This section describes the individual qualities necessary for performance of the job. It gives a rundown of compensable factors to determine the worth and value of the job and outlines the degree of quality required for the particular job under consideration. This factor analysis of the job provides the basic data for evaluating the job and comparing it with other jobs. The job specifications section serves as the employment standards for the job; it tells what knowledge and physical requirements are necessary to do the job satisfactorily.

How to Write a Job Description

The objective in writing your job description is to outline the position briefly yet accurately. The outline must serve as a guide to understanding your present position and must also be useful in selecting your partner and restructuring your job.

The job specification should be as exact as possible. For example, if you are a clerk in the accounting department, your title should be listed as "accounting clerk" rather than just "clerk."

In writing the job summary, try to limit yourself to twenty-five words or less. Job duties should be described in no more than two sentences apiece. In both of the foregoing sections, sentences should begin with *action verbs* (see p. 67) and then describe what is done.

On page 35 is a Job Analysis Questionnaire.

JOB ANALYSIS QUESTIONNAIRE

List: . job title   . immediate supervisor
       . status   . name of person preparing questionnaire
       . location   . name of person who approved it
       . department   . date prepared
              . when updated (if relevant)

JOB SUMMARY: In twenty-five words or less, state your primary
   function -- for example, "Responsible for greeting visitors,
   answering/routing telephone calls, typing correspondence."

JOB DUTIES: State your working procedures -- for example,
   "Sort and deliver mail; maintain office services budget book,
   files for office manager, product clipping book, and telex
   files."

ACCOUNTABILITIES: Describe the results desired -- for example,
   "Corporate visitors receive a pleasant, efficient first impres-
   sion upon entering headquarters office. Smooth office operations
   are ensured through telephone communications."

MATERIALS AND EQUIPMENT: Provide a list of materials and equipment
   the person would normally use -- for example, adding machine, cal-
   culator, computer equipment, computer terminal, CRT, switchboard,
   telephone, transcriber for dictation, typewriter, word processor,
   and "other."

JOB SPECIFICATIONS: Read each question carefully and check the one
   that applies to how you perform your job -- for example, "The
   instructions I get are precise and almost always the same."

1. Extent to which work is performed independently:

   a. Procedures are precise and almost always the same. (1)
   b. Instructions are precise and change only for special
       needs. (2)
   c. I decide what I need to do, get approval, and proceed. (3)
   d. I determine what I need to do; my supervisor may or may
       not check it. (4)
   e. I do my job according to general guidelines and decide
       the methods and tools needed. (5)

2. Supervision exercised:

   a. I supervise no one. (1)
   b. I work in a group; occasionally I assist the others in
       the group. (2)
   c. I supervise one or more people, assign and check their
       work, recommend hires, terminations, and salary adjust-
       ments. (3)
   d. I supervise one or more supervisors and others, recommend
       hires, terminations, and salary adjustments. (4)
   e. I divide my time between supervising other supervisors and
       planning. (5)
   f. I spend most of my time planning and am responsible for
       other supervisors. (6)

3. Authority exercised:

a. I do things exactly as instructed. (1)
b. I change or alternate some of my tasks. (2)
c. I sometimes need people in other departments to give my work priority or to work with me. (3)
d. My work requires that I set priorities. (4)
e. When I set priorities, I get people in other departments to work with me. (5)
f. My work is what I think needs to be done. I get assistance and cooperation from other departments. (6)

4. Confidentiality:

a. I do not work with confidential information. (1)
b. I sometimes work with confidential information. (2)
c. I work with confidential information (such as salaries for grades 1 to 8). (3)
d. I work with and am responsible for sensitive information. (4)
e. I work with and am responsible for information available only to top management. (5)
f. I work with and am responsible for information available only to top policymakers. (6)

5. Difficulty:

a. I encounter no serious difficulties in my job. (1)
b. I perform clerical tasks, see and correct errors. (2)
c. My work varies and involves using an adding machine or type-writer. (3)
d. Records I keep or information I collect is checked shortly after I perform the task. (4)
e. Records I keep or information I collect is not normally checked. (5)
f. I am given general instructions, and I decide how I perform the task. (6)
g. My job involves some problem solving where the data are readily available. (7)
h. I define problems, identify facts, develop conclusions and formulate solutions. (8)

6. Accuracy:

a. I perform ordinary tasks involving little chance of error. (1)
b. I perform tasks where errors are found and easily corrected. (2)
c. I perform tasks where my errors can be found in the next step, but will be a problem to correct. (3)
d. My errors could cause considerable loss of time or money. (4)
e. The tasks I perform are not checked immediately; errors would cause a serious loss of time or money. (5)
f. Errors I make in performance or judgment would cause serious loss of time or money or would embarrass the company and damage its reputation with the public. (6)

7. Financial responsibility:

   a. I handle no cash.
   b. I handle cash up to: ___$500 ___$5,000 ___$10,000 ___any amount
   c. I approve no invoices.
   d. I approve invoices up to: ___$500 ___$5,000 ___$20,000
       ___any amount

8. Personal contacts:

   a. My job requires no particular contact with others. (1)
   b. My job requires contact with just my immediate co-workers and
       supervisor. (2)
   c. My job requires frequent contact about routine matters with
       other departments and requires securing cooperation in solving
       problems.
   d. My job requires regular contact with many people to coordinate
       various activities. (4)
   e. I am in regular contact with others, including the public, to
       coordinate various activities or interpret company policies and
       practices. (5)

9. Education required:

   a. High school. (1)
   b. High school plus about one full year of college or business or
       secretarial school. (2)
   c. Associate degree or at least three full years of college. (3)
   d. Bachelor's degree. (4)
   e. Master's degree. (5)
   f. Ph.D. (6)

10. Experience required:

   a. No experience in particular. (0)
   b. Two years of general experience in an unrelated field. (1)
   c. Four years of general experience or one year of directly
       related experience. (2)
   d. Six years of general experience or two years of directly
       related experience. (3)
   e. Five years of directly related experience. (4)
   f. Eight years of directly related experience. (5)
   g. Ten years of directly related experience. (6)

JOB DESCRIPTION

TITLE: Manager - Administrative Services   STATUS: Exempt
LOCATION: New York Division Headquarters   DATE ORIGINATED: 1/1/74
DEPARTMENT: Administrative Services   DATE: 1/8/81 (revised)
IMMEDIATE SUPERVISOR: Vice President, Admin.   GRADE: 11
WRITEEN BY: Manager - Compensation   SIGNATURE:_____
APPROVED BY: Vice President - Personnel   SIGNATURE:_____

SUMMARY: To coordinate the various administrative activities of the
Division and to facilitate the flow of information within the Divsion
through the use of modern communication techniques.

JOB DUTIES

1. Establish and maintain a Division operating policy and procedures
    manual.
2. Work with Corporate and Division departments in writing and
    securing approval of policies and procedures.
3. Maintain a Division organization manual.
4. Establish and monitor internal organization announcements.
5. Coordinate Division requirements for administrative services at
    headquarters building (office space, duplicating, telephones).
6. Supervise the activities of the Word Processing Center, and
    establish procedures for facilitating the transmission of work
    to and from the Center.
7. Supervise the purchase of office equipment, and maintain an in-
    ventory of all such equipment at Headquarters location.
8. Plan and handle all administrative details of the Division manage-
    ment luncheons and Division management meetings.
9. Manage the Division contributions budget, which involves the co-
    ordination and administration of the activities in this area of all
    Division locations, and review and make recommendations on all re-
    quests received for funds from Division Headquarters contributions
    budget.
10. Undertake other special projects as assigned by the Vice President,
    Administration.

ACCOUNTABILITIES

To provide effective administrative services that ensure the efficient
operation of the Division Headquarters, to facilitate coordination of
Division and Corporate policies and procedures, to aid in the promotion of public-spirited activities.

JOB SPECIFICATIONS

Performs job according to general descriptive terms within overall
policies. Employee develops and prescribes the methods and tools
used. (1-e)

Assigns and directs work performed by one or more persons. Employee
is a first-level supervisor and reviews job performance of persons
supervised; such reviews are part of salary adjustment procedures. (2-c)

Exercises considerable authority to cause time or material resources
to be committed to alternate activities within the scope of the
function. (3-c)

Works with and has access to information of a sensitive nature requiring a high level of confidentiality. (4-d)

Performs tasks that require solving problems; this involves defining
the problem, identifying facts, and developing conclusions. This
work also involves long-range planning. (5-h)

Performs tasks that are neither verified nor checked immediately.
Errors will cause serious loss and embarrass the company. (6-e)

Handles cash in amounts up to $500, and approves invoices up to
$5,000. (7-b and e)

Performs tasks that involve regular contact with others, including
the public, for the purpose of coordinating various activities or
interpreting company policies and practices. (8-e)

Must have an associate degree for completing a specific two-year
program of studies at an accredited college, or must have completed
three years of college courses at an accredited college. (9-c)

Should have six years of general experience in an unrelated field
or two years of experience in a field directly related to the job. (10-d)

JOB DESCRIPTION

TITLE: Receptionist/Typist
LOCATION: Corporate Headquarters
DEPARTMENT: Office Services
IMMEDIATE SUPERVISOR: Office Manager
WRITTEN BY: Office Manager
APPROVED BY: President

STATUS: Nonexempt
DATE ORIGINATED: 12/1/76
DATE: 1/8/81 (revised)
GRADE: 5
SIGNATURE:_____
SIGNATURE:_____

SUMMARY: Responsible for greeting visitors, answering/routing telephone calls, typing Chairman's correspondence and reports. Functions
as Secretary to Office Manager.

JOB DUTIES

1. Sort and deliver mail.
2. Greet visitors, answer/route phone calls, and take messages.
3. Type for Chairman and Office Manager.
4. Maintain Office Services budget book, chronological files for
    Chairman and Office Manager, monthly operating reports, product
    clipping book, and telex files.
5. Prepare expense accounts for Chairman and Office Manager
6. Prepare and route executive travel schedule.
7. Order all office supplies and stationery with direction from
    Office Manager.
8. Send out daily requests for annual reports and interim statements.
9. Maintain/update Corporate mailing lists.
10. Record daily postage meter and request funds when necessary. Main-
    tain updated information on postal procedures, rates and so on.
11. Maintain record of Corporate stock in stock book.
12. Special projects as assigned.

ACCOUNTABILITIES

Aids in ensuring smooth, efficient operation of Corporate Headquarters
office.

JOB SPECIFICATIONS

Performs job according to written or oral instructions for which there
are alternatives employee must recognize. Must consult with supervisor
before choosing alternatives. (1-b)

Performs work at lowest formal level in the department. (2-a)

Has limited authority to cause time or material resources to be committed to alternate activities. (3-b)

Occasionally works with confidential information. (4-b)

Keeps records, and accumulates information using a prescribed system
under close supervision. (5-d)

Performs tasks in which errors detected in next step could significantly
decrease efficiency of next operation. (6-c)

Performs tasks involving routine contact with other departments that
require tact to secure information or resolve difficulties. (8-c)

Must be a high school graduate and have one year of college courses or
a one- or two-year course at a business or secretarial school. (9-b)

Should have two years of general experience in an unrelated field. (10-b)

With this questionnaire as a guide, you will be able to write a complete, up-to-date description of your present position. (Each of the job specifications is followed by a number in parentheses. These numbers are used for weighting purposes in assigning salary grades and do not affect how you write your job description.)

The questionnaire is followed by two typical job descriptions (see pp. 38 and 40). The first, for manager—administrative services, details a somewhat complex job requiring a substantial degree of collaboration and communication; the second, for a receptionist/typist, describes a task-oriented position that will not be difficult to restructure as a shared job. You will utilize both the questionnaire and the job descriptions in analyzing and restructuring your job for sharing.

FINDING A PARTNER

Open communications, professional respect, and flexibility are the keys to successful job sharing. Although many have likened job sharing to marriage, which in some respects may be true, you and your partner need not be buddies to make a shared job work. What you will need is a compatibility born out of shared skills, communications, goals, and respect. Be patient in choosing your partner; you will need a strong commitment both to each other and to the job in order to succeed.

Where to Look and What to Look for

Using your job description and job specifications, establish a profile for your potential partner. You may want to draw up a table like this one used for the job of manager of administrative services. List all those job duties for which specific know-how is important and whether it is required or can be readily learned on the job.

A potential partner may be sitting next to you. Look around.

```
                        PARTNER PROFILE

Experience/Know-How              Required       Trainable

Ability to write policies
   and procedures                   X
Supervisory skills                  X
Budgeting                           X
Meeting planning                                   X
Purchasing equipment                               X
Space planning                                     X

What are the materials and/or equipment utilized in the day-to-day
performance of the job?  Which skills are required; which can readily
be learned on the job?

Materials/Equipment              Required       Trainable

Calculator                                         X
Dictating equipment                                X

What education and experience are required?

Type of Education/Experience        Degree/Years

Associate degree                        ---
General experience (or)              6 years
  Directly related experience        2 years
```

You may already have a partner in mind, or there may be a co-worker in your organization who is also looking to reduce time on the job.

On the other hand, you may have to launch a search. Professional organizations, community clubs, and the career development departments of universities are good places to start. See the

Appendixes (p. 119) for a partial listing of professional associations, and refer to the *Encyclopedia of Associations* for more. Most job-sharing organizations maintain some kind of listing of individuals interested in sharing jobs, and although they will not act as placement agencies, they can point you to others with similar qualifications who are potential candidates for partners. (At present, Workshare, Inc., has a computerized Job Sharers Bank for this purpose.)

You may find that you want to advertise for a partner. The following information on advertising for a partner will provide you with the tools to launch that campaign.

Good places to run your advertisement are local newspapers, trade journals, and college or professional association newsletters.

Be sure when advertising on your own that you make it clear that you are *not* the company. Otherwise, your ad could constitute false advertising and might be construed as a misrepresentation of your employer.

When writing your advertisement, pick out the most significant aspects of your position, and in the interest of creating a synergy*, seek out those talents where you feel you could use a boost!

Explore what you consider the most attractive aspects of your job, and convey them in your ad. Words such as *challenging, stimulating, rewarding* evoke an image of an active, exciting work environment. Try to paint a picture of what your job is like in as few words as possible. Include three or four of the most significant duties, and end with requirements, salary, and benefits. Box numbers are very useful for screening out unsuitable candidates.

---

*synergy: combined action. This term is taken from physiology and chemistry, but its wider use may loosely be characterized by the idea that the whole is greater than the sum of its parts.

Here is a sample ad.

MANAGER
ADMINISTRATIVE SERVICES

Challenging opportunity for experienced administrator to *work less than full time.* I am seeking a partner to share my position at Fortune 500 corporation. Coordinate administrative activities of Division, plan and handle all details of Division management meetings, manage Division contribution budget, and supervise Word Processing Center. Associate degree and 3–5 years' experience required. Good starting salary and generous benefits package. Send résumé and covering letter to Box XYZ.

In effect, you are going to become a mini-personnel department; so after you've developed a profile, you should establish an interviewing guide to use when discussing the shared job with potential partners. Use the following as a guide to conducting your interview; it will give you some idea of topics to cover.

INTERVIEW GUIDE

Work History

Duties   Reasons for changing jobs
Likes/dislikes   Leadership experience
Achievements   Number of previous jobs
Strengths/weaknesses   Factors of job satisfaction
Working conditions   Type of job desired
Level of earnings   Total job accomplishment

Education and Training

Best/poorest subjects
Grades/effort
Extracurricular activities

Special achievements
How was education financed?
Total school achievement

Early Home Background

Parents' occupations
Temperament of parents
Size of family

How strictly raised?
Age of financial independence
Involvement in community

Personality, Motivation, and Character

Maturity
Emotional stability
Team worker
Tact
Adaptability
Self-discipline
Initiative
Sincerity

Follow-through
Confidence
Assertiveness
Conscientiousness
Hard worker
Pride
Honesty

In addition to outlining overall work achievements, the work history should give you some insight into your partner's work attitudes and how well they mesh with yours. A discussion of education and training will give you a chance to investigate aptitudes and perhaps identify some untapped skills. Compatibility is absolutely essential to the success of a job-sharing partnership. Spend some time exploring the maturity, motivation, and general character of the potential candidate. There is no reason to pass judgment on who is right or wrong or better, but it would be wise to ascertain that you are both pretty much on the same track. Get to know each other's personal likes, dislikes, and philosophies.

Remember that there is no reason for you to be mirror images of each other in any way. On the other hand, if there is the slightest suspicion on either side that a real or imagined clash may exist, you must both feel free to withdraw at the very beginning. Continuing to explore a job-sharing program with a less than compatible partner can only lead to self-defeat. Neither of you is bound to maintain the partnership at this initial stage, and now is the time to terminate it, not after you have both invested considerable time and energy.

In sounding out your potential partner, be sure to determine the sense of equality between the two of you. Would you be giving more to the partnership, or would you be busy trying to catch up?

In addition to utilizing the Interview Guide, you should review the "egonomics" of job sharing with potential partners (see p. 21). Make sure the person you finally choose has a clear picture of just what sharing a job is all about. Ultimately, you will want to come up with written documentation for your employer on the synergy that will be created by the two of you sharing the job and how a broader range of talents will be available in that one job title. Your first step in preparing your proposal should be to identify how the two of you complement each other. Draw up a Partnership Profile like the one shown here.

PARTNERSHIP PROFILE

Jane Doe (incumbent)
Work History

2.5 years as Manager of Administrative Services

1 year as Special Assistant to the President

Harry Smith
Work History

2 years as consultant writing policies and procedures

5 years as Office Manager in major law firm

6 years with firm in various
Administrative Assistant positions

Education
Associate Degree

Areas of Expertise
Meeting planning, budget administration, wide knowledge of
overall operations of firm

Part-time job as Front Desk
Clerk in resort hotel during college

Education
Bachelor of Science

Areas of Expertise
Management of large word processing function, hotel experience, policy writing

Once you have chosen your partner, the two of you will be working together to meet the challenge of sharing a job. Having a partner will give you someone to brainstorm with, a mutual support,
and two sets of ideas and experience to draw on.

OTHER POINTS TO CONSIDER

There are four more points you and your partner will need to
cover before approaching your employer: how you will share the
responsibilities, how you will schedule your time, how you will
share fringe benefits, and what communication tools you will em-
ploy.

Sharing Responsibilities

Using your job description, define each partner's areas of strength
and weakness and which are the major and minor responsibilities.
Separate the plums from the pits. Decide which duties would benefit
from collaboration and which tasks could be done by one individual.
Keep in mind those tasks that involve peaks and valleys.

Once again, using the job description for a manager of
administrative services as a model, determine how those responsibilities can be shared. Job duties 1 to 4 require certain writing
skills and an ability to communicate information. It may happen

at a time of management reorganization that there is a flurry of new policies and procedures, coupled with revisions of the organization manual and several organization announcements. Each partner could assume responsibility for certain policies and certain organizational announcements, thus lightening the load on one person and assuring prompt communication of changes to the entire organization. Job duties 5 to 7 require day-to-day attention along with a certain technical knowledge of equipment and new developments. One partner may be stronger in this area than the other; thus, a learning process will occur. Job duty 8, the division management luncheons and division management meetings, entails a myriad of details. There are innumerable bases to be covered, from selecting sites and speakers to planning menus, scheduling transportation, and disseminating information. Two people collaborating on these programs ensures that nothing will fall between the cracks. These same two people will be able to explore new ideas, thereby keeping the format and content of the meetings fresh. Managing the division contributions budget, job duty 9, requires not only certain budgetary expertise but also an objective point of view in making decisions. Again, the benefit of two people working on these decisions will be the assurance of a higher degree of fairness. For the vice president—administration who assigns special projects, it will mean that he or she now has two sets of talents to draw upon.

Establishing an outline of how your job duties will be shared provides your supervisor and management with a clear picture of accountability. It may happen that after the first six or seven months of sharing the job, you find the responsibilities are inequitably distributed. There is no reason why they cannot be reassessed and reworked. It is, however, important that you have a clear idea of how the job is going to be done from the beginning in order to prevent any unnecessary misunderstandings or uncovered bases. Here is a sample of how the sharing of these responsibilities was determined.

JOB DUTY	DIVIDE/COLLABORATE
Communication of policies and organization changes	*Collaborate—institute change, obtain approvals, record steps on flow chart, publish final document*
Day-to-day office services	*Collaborate—maintain records, review requirements daily*
10 monthly management luncheons	*Divide—each partner responsible for 5 luncheons*
Annual management meeting and sales meetings	*Collaborate on management meeting, divide sales meetings (1 each)*
Contributions budget	*Divide budget by regions, collaborate on final budget*
Supervision of word processing center	*Collaborate*

Once you have determined how each of the job duties will be shared, either by collaborating or by dividing, you should demonstrate how the job will benefit from the synergistic effect of job sharing. List each job duty, and briefly describe how it will benefit from job sharing. For example:

JOB DUTY	COMBINED TALENT/SYNERGY
Management meetings	*With two people, less time traveling for each, office can be covered while one is away*
Management luncheons	*Two sets of ideas for speakers and formats, expanded professional contacts*
Day-to-day office service	*Burnout reduced*
Contributions budget	*Two people can check each other's work, eliminates errors*

TIME SCHEDULES

There are many ways to share your time. The two most significant factors are your employer's needs and your own time constraints. The peak periods and lulls will dictate whether you and your partner should overlap, and when. If the job is one involving a great deal of makeready time before the person doing it can get going, full days for each worker will be more efficient than half days. You may decide to work half days, every other day, every other week, or even six months on and six months off. Keep in mind when you prepare your time schedule that your attention to the needs of the job will be a major selling point with your employer. The Sample Time Schedules below show some of the options open to you.

In examining your own time constraints, keep in mind that you may require some flexibility. Will you both be able and willing to cover for each other in an emergency? Is there a high probability that emergencies of the kind requiring an employee to miss work may arise? For example, the parent of very young children or an employee with an invalid relative at home is more likely to have legitimate miss-work emergencies. Is one of you limited by the availability of baby-sitters? Is commuting time a major consideration in planning your schedule? What happens in a snowstorm?

SAMPLE TIME SCHEDULES

The following sample schedules are all based on a five-day work-week and an eight-hour workday.

Sample 1: Each partner works twenty hours a week with no overlap.

	Monday	Tuesday	Wednesday	Thursday	Friday
Morning	A	B	A	B	A
Afternoon	B	A	B	A	B

Sample 2: Each partner works twenty hours a week with one hour overlap each day.

	Monday	Tuesday	Wednesday	Thursday	Friday
Morning	B	B	B	B	B
Afternoon	A	A	A	A	A

Sample 3: Each partner works two and a half days a week with one hour overlap each week.

	Monday	Tuesday	Wednesday	Thursday	Friday
A (A.M.) / B (P.M.)		A	B	A	B

Sample 4: Each partner works two days one week and three days the next, with no overlap.

	Monday	Tuesday	Wednesday	Thursday	Friday
Week 1	B	A	B	A	B
Week 2	A	B	A	B	A

Shared Time Schedules

In establishing your time schedule, you should list each shared job duty and note whether it has any specific time requirements, such as weekly peak activity, summer lull, annual event requiring extra coverage, and hiring of temporary help, and how job sharing will improve coverage of it.

The following is a sample of how this was done for the manager of administrative services:

JOB DUTY	SPECIAL TIME CONSIDERATION	SUGGESTED COVERAGE
1 annual management meeting	*Requires travel, usually 7 to 10 days*	*1 partner handles, other covers office; alternate annually*
2 annual sales meetings	*Require travel, usually 7 to 10 days*	*Each partner handles 1 meeting*
Contributions budget	*Peak activity mid-September*	*Partners both work 1 extra day per week for 2-week period*

DIVIDING THE FRINGE BENEFITS

Needless to say, the most important factor in deciding how to divide the fringe benefits will be to determine whether as part-timers you will still be eligible for them. Let's work with the assumptions that you are eligible and that you will be sharing one full-time employee's set of benefits. These benefits include:

Medical/hospital insurance

Life insurance equal to two times your annual salary

Long-term disability

Pension plan

Profit sharing

Two weeks' vacation

Ten paid holidays

Sick days earned at the rate of one per month

Fringe benefits fall into three major categories: *Statutory* benefits include Social Security (at present, 6.65 percent on the first $29,700 of salary), unemployment insurance (at present, 2.3

percent of first $6,000 of salary), and workers' compensation insurance (at present, $0.85 per $100 of salary). Check with your
local office of the Department of Labor for the most up-to-date
figures. *Compensatory* benefits include sick leave, paid vacation,
and holidays. *Supplementary* benefits include life insurance; hospitalization, major medical, dental, and long-term disability insurance; pension plans, and a variety of other fringes such as tuition reimbursement, stock options, and profit sharing.

With regard to statutory benefits, you have no choice. Compensatory and supplementary benefits should be treated as they
would be if the position were filled by an individual employee.
Some firms choose to provide full benefits for both members of
the job-sharing team. This can drastically inflate the cost of a job-
sharing program and in the long run defeat its purpose. In sharing
one benefits package, you and your partner may opt for dual coverage and share the cost of two sets of benefits with your employer. On the other hand, you may prefer a "cafeteria" approach to benefits. The decision should be reached jointly. Here
is an example of how benefits can be shared.

FRINGE BENEFIT	PARTNER A	PARTNER B
Pension plan	*50%*	*50%*
Life insurance	*50%*	*50%*
Medical insurance		*100%*
Dental insurance	*100%*	

The simplest thing, of course, is to split the benefits right
down the middle, with you and your partner covering the cost of
the additional insurance with your employer. If, for example, the
medical plan for one full-time employee costs your employer $20
per month, the cost to maintain full coverage for each of you
would be $40; therefore you and your partner would each pay
your employer $10 per month to retain your full medical benefits.
You may find, though, that because of family coverage through a

spouse or parent, you have no need of the medical plan and that what you'd really like is some extra vacation time. This point may also be negotiable with your employer. Then, again, your employer may feel that because the firm is absorbing additional Social Security costs, it is not necessary to offer you this negotiable benefit. The most important things for you to know are what your benefits are and what you want.

ESTABLISHING COMMUNICATION TOOLS

Straightforward communications are the most essential tools of successful job sharing. Part of those communications will come about as a result of establishing good systems; however, the best systems in the world won't work if they are not based on underlying trust and honesty. Each of you must keep the other totally informed about what is happening.

Sometimes when tasks are divided rather than shared, it is merely necessary to let your partner know that a certain project is under way and has reached a certain point. Where the task is collaborative, however, complete information is essential for one partner to continue where the other left off. Anything short of complete information will undermine your partner's efforts—and the job-sharing program.

Job sharers have utilized many means of communication to ensure the smooth operation of their job. Here are some examples.

Telephone Log: Each partner keeps a brief listing of incoming and outgoing phone calls, including whom to or from, telephone number, and purpose of call.

Chronological File: An extra copy of all correspondence generated by each partner is kept in a chronological file. The partners review the file each day to see what was sent out the day before.

Daily Correspondence Log: Any correspondence that is routed before both partners have reviewed it should be either logged or copied and a notation made explaining its disposition.

Tape Recordings: In place of lengthy notes, many job sharers keep a tape recorder at hand to let partners know of the day's activities. This is also an excellent means of letting each other know what went on at meetings without establishing intricate briefing procedures. You can just tape the whole meeting!

The Red Folder: This folder contains items that require the immediate attention of the partner on duty.

Daily, Weekly, or Monthly Folder Meetings: Folders are established for each partner that contain items requiring person-to-person review on a noncritical basis (as opposed to the items in the red folder).

Daily or Weekly Telephone Conferences: One team of job sharers holds their telephone conferences while feeding their babies!

In addition to establishing procedures for communicating with each other, the job-sharing team will need to keep on top of communications with their supervisor. Three effective tools are:

A Supervisor's Folder: Each partner puts a copy of any correspondence or notes regarding conversations with their supervisor into this folder. This ensures that neither partner has missed anything.

Weekly, Biweekly, or Monthly Staff Meetings: Both partners and their supervisor attend, or if that's not feasible, a conference call is placed.

Weekly Activities Reports to the Supervisor: Both partners prepare and sign a report describing what has been accomplished that week and any critical items that are upcoming.

In establishing the communication tools for your shared job, you can follow the model below. The list covers each job duty, whether it will be shared collaboratively or split, and the type of communication tool to be used (e.g., tape recordings, telephone logs).

JOB DUTY	TYPE OF SHARING	COMMUNICATION TOOL
Policies and procedures	*Collaborate*	*Flow Chart*
Day-to-day office services	*Collaborate*	*Red Folder, Tape Recorder*
Monthly management luncheons	*Divide*	*Each partner maintains clear records, accessible to the other in case of emergency*

You should also indicate specific accountabi lities to your supervisor and how they are to be communicated (e.g., weekly meetings, activities report, joint or individual communication).

ACCOUNTABILITY	COMMUNICATION TOOL
Day-to-day office services	*Activities report*
Management meetings	*Monthly meeting, carbon copies of all correspondence*

3

Twoing It

*Applying for a New Job
to Be Shared*

There are a variety of ways to approach applying for a shared job. You can first find a partner and then tackle the job hunt jointly, or you can go it alone, working on the assumption that there may already be someone on the staff of your potential employer who is looking to cut back to less than full-time employment.

In either case, you will need a good résumé, a covering letter, and a sound foundation in the ways in which you plan to share a job. This chapter provides you with the tools to write a good résumé singly and then jointly, single and joint covering letters, and a basic interviewing outline. Time scheduling, benefit sharing, task splitting, and communication tools should all be worked out in advance, and questions anticipated and answered.

YOUR RÉSUMÉ

To begin with, you will need to write your autobiography—the foundation for your résumé. The following typical autobiography, or résumé inventory, will help you assess your skills and achievements.

RÉSUMÉ INVENTORY

EDUCATION

High school If you are a college graduate, you will probably not
use this information on your résumé, but you may need it for
application forms.
   School, dates attended, type of diploma, and date of graduation
   Major studies, class standing, best subjects
   Honors and awards, extracurricular achievements

College
   School, dates attended, type of diploma, and date of graduation
   Major studies, class standing, best subjects
   Honors and awards, extracurricular achievements

Graduate School
   School, dates attended, type of diploma, and date of graduation
   Major studies, class standing, best subjects
   Honors and awards, extracurricular achievements

Note: If the college or graduate school is not well known, be sure
to point out its relevance to the job, if possible.

School jobs
   Indicate whatever jobs you held during your school years and how
   much of your education you financed yourself.

EMPLOYMENT

   Make a list of every major position you have held, even those with
   the same employer. Include at least one accomplishment for each
   position. Start with your earliest job, and work up to your present
   position. (This order will be reversed if you chose to do a chronological résumé.)

OTHER TRAINING

Make a list of any training you have received in addition to your
formal education. Be sure to include on-the-job seminars you may
have attended, adult education courses, military training, or
training you received as part of a volunteer activity. List each
one separately, indicating:
    Name of course
    When taken
    Skills learned
    Credits accumulated (if any)

COMMUNITY AND HOME WORK

Many activities at home and in the community add to your experience
and can provide training that is applicable in the job market. Make
a list of your community activities and anything you do at home that
could be applied to the workplace.

HOBBIES

Your hobbies can also reveal special skills. Make a list of them,
indicating how long you have been interested in each, what kind of
training was required, and any special accomplishments.

PROFESSIONAL ASSOCIATIONS, HONORS, AWARDS

Make a list of the honors and awards you have received and the
professional associations you belong to.

MISCELLANEOUS

Review everything you have listed. Is there anything else you
would like to say about yourself? Something you are particularly
proud of? This may well demonstrate a skill that can be applied
to the job.

REFERENCES

Your references will not appear on your resume, but you should
prepare a list of four or five people (preferably professional
contacts) who will give you a good reference. Write or call each
of them to ask if you may use their names and alert them to when
to expect a contact from a prospective employer.

Once you have completed your autobiography, you are ready to write a résumé. Remember, the average résumé receives approximately thirty seconds attention from your targeted employer. Be as succinct as possible. In all cases, try to stick to one page. Highlight your experience and skills; you can embellish at the interview.

There are two basic résumé styles: functional and chronological. The functional résumé is particularly useful to highlight a variety of skills acquired from various jobs, if you have a broken work history or volunteer experience that you want to feature, or if you are looking to switch specialties. This résumé style also lends itself well to joint résumés. Chronological résumés highlight direct experience, a solid background in the field, continuous employment, and an impressive record.

One new résumé style is the focused résumé, which I developed for my own clients. This résumé combines a highlight of experience at the beginning of the résumé with a more traditional chronological résumé. Pick out the three things (no more than three) you have listed on your résumé that you want a prospective employer to focus on. List these three functions at the top of your résumé, next to "Experience." If there are different areas you are interested in, you can use the same chronological résumé and change the "Experience" line to suit the job you're after. See page 66 for an example of the focused résumé.

Following are résumé rules for functional and chronological résumés, a list of action verbs, and a list of functional titles. Each set of résumé rules is followed by sample résumés. You may want to try both styles to see which fits your experience best.

Functional Résumé Rules

Use a separate paragraph to highlight each particular area of expertise or involvement.

Arrange the paragraphs in order of importance. Start with the areas most related to your job target.

Stress the accomplishments that are most related to your job target.

Emphasize particular abilities that are important to that target.

Remember that you can include accomplishments and experience that relate to nonpaid work—for example, administration of a fund-raising campaign or designing an advertising program for a charity bazaar. If you did the work and achieved the results, you can include it.

Education, if it is very recent, can be placed at the beginning. If it's not recent, list it at the end.

Briefly list actual work experience in the same style as for a chronological résumé: dates, employer, and title.

Do *not* exceed one page in length.

Avoid gimmicks such as drawings, unusual colors, difficult-to-read type styles.

Use good paper, preferably a cream or very light gray stock, and make sure that the printing job is clear and clean.

Here is an outline of how to draft a functional résumé.

Functional Résumé Drafting Form

Function Title: *Action Research*

Write down all achievements, accomplishments, or results of any kind that you have produced in your work. Include nonwork experience and school or community activities. For example:

I set up meetings with groups of people to solve problems and then chaired the meetings and summarized the results. I talked to the individuals and looked at how they behaved in the meetings.

Now review what you have written, highlighting the most relevant information. By utilizing the lists of action verbs (p. 67) and functional headings (p. 68), you can translate that information to:

Designed, moderated/conducted, and analyzed focus group sessions, in-depth interviews, and participant-observation episodes.

The functional résumé that follows illustrates how the finished product should look.

Chronological Résumé Rules

Start with your most recent employment, and work backward. Emphasize your most recent employment *if* that's the area you plan to stay in.

Detail the last three or four positions. If you held several positions with one firm, list each one separately. If your first few positions are somewhat irrelevant to your present goal, use words such as *progressed from* to indicate that you moved up the ladder.

Dates of employment should be listed by years, not months and days.

Briefly describe your employer—for example, "Fortune 500 manufacturer" or "distributor of widgets, with multimillion-dollar annual sales."

If specific functions within several positions are the same, do not repeat them for each listing.

Stress the major accomplishments and responsibilities for each position.

FUNCTIONAL RÉSUMÉ

OBJECTIVE: Position in market research, staff or consultant, to
design, moderate/conduct, and analyze focus group sessions
and in-depth interviews.

SUMMARY

ACTION RESEARCH: Designed, moderated/conducted, and analyzed
focus group sessions, in-depth interviews, and participant-
observation episodes.

TRAINING AND PRESENTATION: Organized and conducted training
conferences using group process techniques: problem solving,
task analysis, instrumented exercises. Conducted orientation
sessions for subjects of field studies, users of new systems,
and college students. Presented papers at professional conferences and seminars. Was instructor of college sociology
courses.

PROJECT COORDINATION: Coordinated regular weekend and all-day
conferences. Organized political fund-raising events and
rallies. Coordinated direct-mail fund-raising and analyzed
returns.

EMPLOYMENT HISTORY

1980-Present   Management Analyst
               Office of the Budget, City of New York

1976-1979   Administrative Associate
               Vernon Menswear, New York, New York

1974-1976   Assistant Director
               St. Botolph's University, Olean, New York

1973-1974   Research Associate
               Berdon Laboratories, New York, New York

EDUCATION

Ph.D., Sociology/Social Psychology, St. Botolph's University, 1974
Certificate in Organizing Skills, Long Island School of Business
    Administration, 1981
Languages: German, Spanish, and Swedish

PROFESSIONAL AFFILIATIONS

American Sociology Association
Organization Development Network

When describing previous positions, emphasize the details most relevant to your present job target.

Education should be at the bottom of the page unless it is very recent.

Keep the résumé to one page in length.

Here is an outline of how to draft a chronological résumé.

```
                    CHRONOLOGICAL RÉSUMÉ DRAFTING FORM

Dates:  _____  to  _____

Position:  _____

Employer:  _____

List accomplishments or results that describe your performance in
that position:

_____

_____

_____

_____

_____


Now review what you have written.  By condensing the information,
targeting your next job, and utilizing action verbs, that infor-
mation can be rewritten for a résumé.

_____

_____

_____
```

The following chronological résumé illustrates how the finished product should look.

CHRONOLOGICAL RÉSUMÉ

BUSINESS EXPERIENCE

1976- Lambert Brothers, New York, Consulting Engineers
Present   Position: Accounting Manager
Responsible for all accounting functions, including preparation of financial statements, EEOC compliance reports,
and contract analysis and compliance. Designated company
liaison with all clients. Designed and implemented reporting system for firm's principals, resulting in significantly improved monitoring of engineering projects. Participated in management meetings with firm's principals;
recommended and implemented actions in the financial area.

1974-1976 Marston Interiors, New York, Furniture Importer
          Position: Accountant/Office Manager
Responsible for monitoring all day-to-day internal operations. Hired and supervised clerical staff, managed workload, and evaluated performance. Dealt with clients in
person and on the telephone. Selected suppliers, negotiated service agreements. Established and designed office
policies and procedures. Other responsibilities included
all accounting functions and maintenance of open letter-
of-credit ledger.

1956-1974 Harvey Plastics, New York, Fortune 500 Manufacturer
          Position: Progressed from Trainee, Controller's
                    Department, to Cashier

  1966-1974 Cashier: Cash management of all corporate funds.
  Expense forecasting, reports of cash flow. Developed system resulting in improved control of expense account reporting and compliance with IRS standards.

  1962-1964 Accounts Payable Supervisor

  1959-1962 Accounts Receivable Supervisor
  Responsible for supervision of five to six clerks, data
  processing input, developed standardized form letters
  for vendor/customer correspondence, preparation of
  monthly activity reports.

  1956-1959 Trainee, Controller's Department
  Was exposed to various aspects of accounting group,
  accounts receivable, accounts payable, general ledger
  and payroll.

EDUCATION
  Hunter College, New York City
  Sales Analysis Institute, Inc. (diploma)

ORGANIZATIONS
  American Consulting Engineers Council
  New York Association of Consulting Engineers

FOCUSED RÉSUMÉ

EXPERIENCE: Bookkeeping/Accounting, Office Management, and
   Customer Relations

1978-Present   Bowden's, New York
                 Office Manager/Bookkeeper
   Managed office/bookkeeping functions for multimiliion-dollar
   international mink coat manufacturing firm. Responsible for
   accounts payable/receivable, payroll, monthly statements, bank
   records, monthly sales reports, and annual customer analysis.
   Designed schedule for notes payable/receivable. Worked directly
   with major customers both in person and on the telephone.

1974-'78   Hallam's Liquors, New York, New York
                Accountant, Inventory Accounting
   Completely responsible for all inventory control of general wine
   and spirits selling company's domestically produced case goods with
   volume of approximately $2 million monthly. Also responsible for
   computer runs on sales to be posted in control ledger and for tie
   out of the control ledger into final transaction computer run.

1963-'74   Rosenkrantz Children's Wear, New York, New York
                Junior Accountant, Corporate Cost Accounting Department
   Responsible for monthly closing, journalizing information from
   manufacturing locations, and preparing monthly variance summaries,
   insurance reports, controlling company standard cost system data,
   handling of interbranch transfers, assisting in the analysis of
   inventory and variance accounts. Compiled and organized cost
   information for Cost Supervisor, including cost of sales reports,
   overhead cost reports, and other branch and corporate information.

1962-'63   Norwich Advertising, New York, New York
                Clerk Typist, Traffic Department

1961-'62   Tapper & Kirkpatrick, Jersey City, New Jersey
                Office Manager/Receptionist

EDUCATION: Jersey City State College, Jersey City, New Jersey
            Completed two years of Bachelor of Arts studies

OTHER ACTIVITIES: Metropolitan Singers/Greek Chorale Society
                   New York, New York
                   (1973-Present) Toured Greece for three weeks in
   1977, sponsored by the government of Greece and Greek Archdiocese.
   Perform annual concert at Avery Fisher Hall and various other con-
   certs throughout the Greater New York metropolitan area and the
   Boston area.

ACTION VERBS

Administer Manage or direct the execution of affairs.

Advise Recommend a course of action; offer an informed opini on based upon specialized knowledge.

Analyze Separate into elements and critically examine.

Appraise Give an expert judgment of worth or merit.

Approve Accept; exercise final authority with regard to commitment.

Assemble Collect or gather together in a predetermined order .

Authorize Approve; empower through vested authority.

Collaborate Work jointly with; cooperate with others.

Compile Put together information; collect from other documents.

Conduct Carry on; direct the execution of.

Control Measure, interpret, and evaluate actions for conform ance with plans or desired results.

Coordinate Regulate, adjust, or combine the actions of other s to attain harmony.

Correlate Establish a reciprocal relationship.

Delegate Commission another to perform tasks or duties.

Design Conceive, create, and execute according to plan.

Develop Disclose, discover, perfect, or unfold a plan or ide a.

Devise Come up with something new.

Direct Guide work operations through the establishment of objectives, policies, rules, practices, methods, and standards.

Disseminate Spread or disperse information.

Evaluate Determine or fix the value of.

Expedite Accelerate the process or progress of.

Implement Carry out; execute a plan or program.

Initiate Start or introduce.

Investigate Study through close examination and systematic inquiry.

Issue Put forth or distribute officially.

Negotiate Confer with others with an eye to reaching agreement.
Operate Perform an activity or series of activities.
Plan Devise or project the realization of a course of action.
Process Subject something to special treatment; handle in accordance with prescribed procedure.
Recommend Advise or counsel a course of action.
Research Inquire into a specific matter using several sources.
Supervise Personally oversee, direct, or guide the work of others.

FUNCTIONAL HEADINGS

The following list will give you an idea of various functional headings. For more, consult the U.S. Department of Labor's *Dictionary of Occupational Titles*.

Accounting	Drafting	Medicine
Acquisition	Electronics	Navigation
Administrative	Employment	Organization
Advertising	Engineering	Planning
Architecture	Finance	Presentation
Aviation	Fund raising	Printing
Boating	Graphic design	Product development
Career	Inspecting	Production
development	Interviewing	Programming
Chemistry	Instruction	Promotion
Communication	Investigation	Public relations
Community	Investment	Public speaking
affairs	Layout	Publicity
Construction	Legal	Purchasing
Counseling	Management	Real estate
Culinary	Market research	Research
Data processing	Materials	Retailing
Design	handling	Scheduling

Secretarial	Supervision	Teaching
Selling	Systems and	Testing
Social work	procedures	Writing and editing

It will probably take three or four attempts before you are satisfied with your finished résumé. Some of the checkpoints to be considered are:

Have you made any spelling or typing errors?

Are sentences and paragraphs short and to the point?

Is the writing concise and direct?

Have redundancies and repetitions been eliminated?

Are all major time periods covered?

Is layout professional and attractive?

Are accomplishments easily understood?

A few other do's and don't's: Don't list a lot of personal information such as hobbies, fraternal organizations; do indicate extracurricular activities. If you financed your own education, be sure to indicate that. Do this by adding a short sentence at the end of the "Education" section such as, "Completely financed education while attending school full (part) time."

This is the point at which you should include your partner in your planning. Your partner also needs a résumé, preferably one in the same style as yours; it will be too confusing for an employer to relate to two different résumé styles when considering your job-sharing proposal.

Now is also the time to decide the issue of joint versus individual résumés and/or joint covering letters. Unless you intend to prepare a separate résumé for each job applied for, the covering letter is the better route. Your existing résumés cover the background and experience; the letter explains the why of sharing the job. In the case of the joint résumé, be sure that your covering letter briefly explains what job sharing is and that you are both conversant with the techniques of sharing a job and have thoroughly researched the pros and cons, ins and outs. The employer only wants to fill the position, not create a new program. You should therefore be able to slip into the slot with the same ease, training requirements, and so on of a single new employee. This may well mean that your first couple of weeks in the new position will require extra effort. Let your potential employer know that you are aware of this and are willing to expend that effort. Always keep in mind the specific requirements of the job applied for and why together you will do it better than one person could.

A sample joint résumé is presented on page 72.

COVERING LETTERS

Your covering letter should be addressed directly to the person with whom you want the interview. Prior to writing your letter, call the company, and ask the switchboard operator for the name of the person in charge of the department you are interested in— for example, the vice president of sales. Be sure to ask for the correct spelling of the name.

Make your letter special. Mention something particularly pertinent to that person or organization, perhaps something recently mentioned in the press or a new product you have tried, something to get the reader's interest.

It's also very important to make *yourself* special. Mention a reason why the reader should be particularly interested in seeing you. Some research on the firm should provide you with a target to relate your experience to. (Sources for this kind of information are listed in the Appendixes.)

Make sure you use the jargon of the industry you are approaching. Every field has its own language; read some trade journals and articles to familiarize yourself with the way people in that industry express themselves. Be sure you understand exactly what is meant by the use of seemingly common words. When in doubt, don't use them. A sample joint covering letter follows the joint résumé.

JOINT INTERVIEWS

No matter how many job interviews you've been on, it's still a stressful undertaking. One big plus with job sharing is that now you have someone to share the anxiety with.

Some bottom-line basics for any job interview are:

Always be on time (five minutes early is better).

Check your "packaging"—shoes shined, blouse or shirt pressed, clean shaven, neat makeup and hairdo.

Don't fidget. Be sure to wear something comfortable and easy to sit and stand in; carry papers in a briefcase or large envelope.

Put your interviewer at ease. Start the interviewer talking, and then listen, listen, listen.

I strongly recommend that you rehearse your interview, either with a friend or by utilizing a *research and referral interview.* Simply stated, a research and referral interview is when you approach an employer, not for a job, but for suggestions on where to look for a job and how to go about it. This is a wonderful way to hone your interviewing skills, especially where there will be two

JOINT RÉSUMÉ

John Smith
123 Main Street
New York, New York 10032
(212) 798-3102

Jane Doe
456 Avenue A
New York, New York 10012
(212) 456-7898

POSITION APPLIED FOR: Advertising Production Manager

EXPERIENCE

January, 1977-Present
Direct Mail Marketing Manager
ABC Widget Company, New York

May, 1973-August, 1979
Art Director
XYZ Publishing Co., New York

Design and administer direct-mail
marketing program aimed at special
consumer market of 200,000 on a
quarterly basis. Select and order
mailing lists, supervise print
production and lettershop operations and develop cost analysis
and control methods for overall
program.

Managed art department and
supervised four book designers.
Recruited and placed free-lance
artists for special projects.
Negotiated contracts with
outside suppliers. Approved
all final artwork, paste-ups
and jacket designs. Worked
with authors on design requirements.

April, 1976-January, 1977
Advertising Assistant
ABC Widget Company, New York

February, 1972-May, 1973
Assistant to Production Manager
GHI Typesetting Company, New York

Wrote copy and worked with product
managers in determining approach
to various markets.

Aided manager in supervising
production, worked with type-
setters and design staff.

March, 1975-April, 1976
Copywriter
Jones Advertising Agency, New York

Progressed from junior to senior
copywriter on two major accounts.

EDUCATION

B.S., Marketing, City College of
New York, 1974, magna cum laude

B.A., Fine Arts, Art Institute of
Chicago, 1972.
Special courses in graphics and
publishing.

SAMPLE JOINT COVERING LETTER

November 17, 1983

(Inside address)

Dear _____:

The enclosed resumes are in response to your advertisement for a
Career Planning Coordinator in the November 16, 1983 issue of
The Gazette. Our résumés are submitted to fill this position on
a job-sharing basis.

Our combined skills, educations, and business backgrounds offer
the unique opportunity to tap a wide range of talent not usually
found in a single applicant.

By combining the abilities of a proven career counselor at a
major educational institution with the business acumen of a
seasoned personnel administrator of a large corporation, your
firm will enjoy the benefit of two professionals dedicated to
achieving your corporate goals.

Job sharing has been successfully applied in many organizations
desirous of improving productivity, reducing turnover and absenteeism, achieving greater flexibility in work scheduling, and
benefiting from the opportunity to recruit from a broader labor
pool.

We have thoroughly researched the techniques of sharing a job
and are convinced that as Career Planning Coordinator in your
firm we will make a significant contribution to your Human
Resources Development staff.

We look forward to meeting with you to explore this opportunity
further.

Sincerely,

Mary Smith
(address and phone number)

John Cooper
(address and phone number)

Enclosures

of you. It also provides an opportunity to get some objective third-party feedback on your approach.

If you rehearse the job interview with a friend, be sure to do it in the most formal setting possible. Dress as you would for the real interview, set up an exact interview time, and bring your résumés. Allow about an hour for the interview. If possible, use a tape recorder. Here are some sample questions you can anticipate. Some of the questions relate directly to job sharing; others are standard interviewing questions.

Why do you want to work here?

What interests you most about this position?

What are the advantages of job sharing?

Where do you want to be five years from now?

How is job sharing different from part-time work?

How will the two of you handle travel requirements?

Does either of you have any health problems?

Do you know of any examples of job sharing in this type of work?

What happens when one or both of you want to return to full-time work?

What if one of you quits?

How will you handle vacation time?

What are your greatest accomplishments?

Who is really responsible for the job getting done?

How will you cover attendance at meetings?

How are we to handle performance reviews, promotions, and salary increases?

Why don't you want to work full time?

What is your experience for this job?

Have you worked together before?

How long have you known each other?

How did you meet?

What happens if we want to convert the job back to one full-time employee?

How will you handle training?

What contributions will you make to the company?

You may want to ask the interviewer some of the following questions:

Why is this job vacant?

Has the opening been posted in-house?

May we see the job description?

What are the biggest problems in this job?

What are the company's goals?

Where is this job on the organization chart?

How many people do we supervise?

What is expected of the new employee?

Do you have any further questions for us?

After your first rehearsal, listen to the tape, solicit criticism from your interviewer, and if necessary, rehearse again.

Now you're ready for the real thing! Bring your résumés to

the interview. You can never be sure that the interviewer still has the copies you sent with your covering letter. Also bring along one or two articles on job sharing that you can leave with the interviewer as backup on the job-sharing concept.

Impress upon the interviewer that the employer will be getting two sets of talents for the price of one. You and your partner should know ahead of time how you plan to field questions. Now is the time to demonstrate how well you work together. Stepping on each other's lines will turn the interviewer off; so will too much deference. You should feel comfortable saying, "Mary is really the expert in that area; I'm more experienced in this aspect of the job." (All can be lost if Mary turns around and says, "Oh, no, *you* are!") Be sure you're both aware of working back and forth; it's a little like bidding at bridge.

You and your partner must be absolutely clear on how to plan to share the job—the time, the responsibilities, and the benefits (subject to the employer's approval). Consider the questions the interviewer may ask about coverage during an illness, vacations, and the like. Will you both be available to double up for training? Be prepared for a certain amount of skepticism on the part of the interviewer. Above all, don't get defensive. Remember you have every right to want to share a job. On the other hand, the interviewer has the right to decide not to hire a team to fill the job. That's the chance you're taking.

BIBLIOGRAPHY: CAREER PLANNING

Books

Adams, Robert Lang, and Bob Adams, ed. *The Metropolitan New York Job Book.* New York: Bob Abrams, Inc., 1981.

Boll, Carl R. *Executive Jobs Unlimited.* New York: Macmillan Publishing Co., 1980.

Bolles, Richard N. *The Three Boxes of Life.* Berkeley, Calif.: Ten Speed Press, 1981.

_____*What Color Is Your Parachute?* Rev. ed. Berkeley, Calif.: Ten Speed Press, 1982.

Fialer, Howard. *The Complete Job Search Handbook.* New York: Holt, Rinehart & Winston, 1979.

Jackson, Tom. *The Perfect Résumé.* Garden City, N.Y.: Doubleday Publishing Co., Anchor Press, 1980.

_____ and D. Mayleas. *The Hidden Job Market for the Eighties.* New York: Times Books, 1981.

Kline, Linda, and Lloyd L. Feinstein, *Career Changing: The Worry-Free Guide.* Boston: Little, Brown & Co., 1982.

Montrose, David H., and Christopher J. Shinkmon. *Career Development in the 1980's: Theory and Practice.* Springfield, Ill.: Charles C. Thomas Publisher, 1982.

Mormon, Stephen K., and John F. McLoughlin. *Out Interviewing the Interviewers: A Job Winner's Script for Success.* Englewood Cliffs, N.J.: Prentice-Hall, 1983.

Pettus, Theodore T. *One on One.* New York: Random House, 1981.

Rinella, Richard J., and Claire Robbins. *Career Power!: A Manual for Personal Career Advancement.* New York: Amacom, 1980.

Rust, H. Lee. *Job Search: The Complete Manual for Jobseekers.* New York: Amacom, 1981.

Wright, John W. *The American Almanac of Jobs and Salaries.*
New York: Avon Books, 1982.

Articles

"Career Development." *Training and Development Journal*
(February, 1982): entire issue.
Leach, John. "The Career Planning Process." *Personnel Journal* (April 1981).
Levenson, Ann M. "Ten Psychological Roadblocks to Job
Hunting." *Journal of College Placement* (Fall 1982).

Newsletters

Career Development Bulletin (quarterly). New York: Columbia
University, 814 Uris Hall, New York, NY 10027.
Careerism Newsletter. Information Services, Inc., Box 10046,
Rochester, NY 14610.
Daily Plan-It, 38 East Fifty-seventh Street, New York, NY
10022.

4

Fifty-five Is the Speed Limit, Not the Age Limit

That's what the sign over the desk says. And a visit with Evelyn Smith and Sylvia Corvo explains why. Evelyn (65) and Sylvia (72) are the job sharers who administer the Retirees' Job Bank for the Travelers Corporation of Hartford. As one co-worker put it, "They work together like hot fudge on vanilla ice cream: Each one's great alone, but the combination is something special." This team of dynamos both returned to Travelers after retirement to co-direct the job bank. Evelyn Smith retired from Travelers as assistant director of employment in 1979. She enjoyed her two years of retirement, spending time with her family and working with a temporary employment agency to develop a program for hiring senior citizens; but when Travelers invited her back, she was more than willing to take up the challenge. Evelyn's first assignment was to find herself a partner to share her job.

Job sharing is definitely the most efficient way to return older workers to the work force. Of today's retirees who are employed, 69 percent are working on a part-time basis by choice.

Given the fact that the postwar "baby boom" children are moving into their middle life, the need for more flexible work arrangements for older workers will increase dramatically over the next twenty years. Census Bureau figures indicate that the number of new workers in the 18-to-24-year-old bracket will de-

79

crease by 16 percent by the year 2000. In that same period, the segment of the population over 65 will increase by 28 percent. Unless employers accommodate the needs of their older workers by designing more flexible work schedules, they will fall short of their requirements for skilled labor.

Job sharing provides a means of creating part-time employment for these older workers without causing havoc in the workplace. Time schedules, tasks, and compensation for each position can remain the same while serving the needs of workers for reduced work schedules.

Sylvia Corvo was the perfect person to share Evelyn Smith's job. Sylvia retired from Travelers after forty-five years of service, delighted to have the time to see the world. In seven years, you can do a lot of globe-trotting: Florida, the Caribbean islands, California, Hawaii, Austria, Germany, Switzerland, most of the states in the United States, and just about every major capital in Europe. Now Sylvia still has enough time—and income—to travel while also doing a job she enjoys and the added pleasure of friendships at Travelers.

Evelyn and Sylvia share their job fifty-fifty, with one partner working three days one week and two days the next. They cover for each other during vacations and absences. Both are committed to getting the job done, and flexibility is their key. Their job-sharing arrangement has an interesting history.

In August 1980, Morrison Beach, then chairman of the board, announced that Travelers was initiating a national leadership program designed to address the needs and aspirations of older Americans. One aspect of that effort was the development of programs for Travelers own older employees.

To begin with, Travelers surveyed employees aged 55 and over for their opinions of what would be helpful in designing future company programs.*

*Lloyd D. Marquardt and Alice R. Gold, *The Travelers Preretirement Opinion Survey—Report of Results* (Hartford, Conn., January 1981).

The following are among the major findings of the survey:

Of those surveyed, 85 percent expressed an interest in some form of paid employment after they retired. The majority (53 percent) said they would prefer part-time employment with Travelers.

Forty-one percent said they would consider retiring earlier if part-time work were available.

Working fewer days per week is clearly the preferred part-time schedule.

Thirty-nine percent indicated an interest in pursuing a second career. This interest was lowest among weekly employees (32 percent) and highest among officers (56 percent).

Only 9 percent of those surveyed chose volunteer work as their first preference after retirement. An additional 40 percent had some interest in volunteer work, but not as a first choice.

Reasons given for working beyond age 65 were largely economic, although some planned to continue for the enjoyment of work.

A second survey was sent to a sample of Travelers retirees. Included in this sample were all Travelers retirees who were working on a part-time basis for the company and a 20-percent sample of the remaining retirees who were less than 75 years old. Here are some highlights from the second survey, especially as it relates to employment:

A total of 87 percent of the retirees enjoy their retirement, 5 percent dislike retirement, and 8 percent neither enjoy nor dislike retirement.

Interest in postretirement employment among retirees is fairly high; 62 percent expressed interest in working, whereas only 36 percent said they definitely were not interested in postretirement employment.

Of this sample, 21 percent reported that they work for Travelers, 10 percent work for other companies, and 69 percent are not currently employed.

Financial considerations appear to play an important role in the decision to work after retirement. However, other reasons such as deriving a sense of accomplishment, being with people, and providing something to do with their time were also cited as influencing the decision to work after retirement.

A small majority (52 percent) prefer a fixed work schedule after retirement; 40 percent prefer to be on call as needed.

Most working retirees are not interested in working additional hours; 73 percent prefer to work the same number of hours in the future as they currently do.

The median number of hours currently worked per month by retirees is 62.5 hours.

For the most part, working retirees appear content with postretirement employment; 95 percent indicated that overall they are satisfied with postretirement employment.

Utilizing the survey information, Travelers set out to design a program responsive to the needs of its older workers. Retirees would be perfect for shared jobs and for part-time and temporary assignments. On average, the Travelers home office employs sixty to seventy temporary employees per day. The company could afford to pay its retirees more than they might earn through a commercial temporary agency and still save enough on agency fees to pay for the administration of the program. Retirees would be paid at the midpoint of the salary grade for the job they were performing.

The first step for Travelers was to revise its pension plan, which had allowed retirees to work a certain number of hours a month, to one that allows for 960 hours a year. This number was arrived at to keep the program within ERISA regulations and still allow for the fact that the average temporary assignment in the firm lasted three weeks, too long for the monthly allocation previously allowed by the pension plan. Once this revision was completed, letters were sent to all Travelers retirees inviting those who were interested to sign up for temporary and part-time jobs. Finally, the job bank was established.

Each of the retirees registered with the job bank has an enrollment card. Department heads submit job orders to Evelyn or Sylvia, who call those retirees qualified for that particular job. If the first one isn't available, they continue down the list. The retiree is billed to the Personnel Department payroll. At the end of the week, the payroll is allocated to the department employing that retiree. In some cases, a retiree can spend half the day working for one department at one pay rate and the other half in another department at another pay rate.

Most returning Travelers retirees indicated that they would prefer to continue in the type of work they had been doing before retirement. However, because Travelers uses state-of-the-art technology, many assignments require keyboard knowledge, a familiarity with CRTs and IBM's Displaywriter. To bring their retirees up to date, Travelers established a CRT/Displaywriter training course especially for older workers.

At present, over 60 percent of the temporary positions at the Travelers home office in Hartford are filled by retirees, some working for just a short stint of a day or two and others for several weeks or months at a time.

During the Retirees' Job Bank's first year of operation,

Evelyn and Sylvia filled over 700 positions from a pool of more than 500 Travelers retirees.

One of Travelers long-term retired workers is Leslie Bingham. He enthusiastically informed me, "It's better the second time around!" Leslie spent thirty-seven years in the Shipping/Receiving Department of Travelers and held down a job at night, too. Now he's working on converting a particular type of policy from one computer system to another. According to Leslie, "What keeps people going isn't being home sitting down; it's moving." Leslie's supervisor is happy to have him back at work, too; she finds a reservoir of experience, fresh ideas, and enthusiasm that adds to department performance.

When Marian Reinholz stopped by the office to have coffee last July, she was not expecting the birthday bash staged by the Group Pensions Department in honor of her eightieth birthday. Marian retired from Travelers in December 1967. After retirement, she worked as a volunteer with the Heart Association and for cerebral palsy and visited with her children and grandchildren. By the time the job bank started up in 1981, Marian was itching to get back into harness—and back she is, five hours a day, five days a week during the colder months of the year. In the warmer months, she turns her job over to a student so that she can relax and enjoy life.

Last year, Evelyn Smith had an opportunity to prove that history repeats itself. She interviewed and hired Ida Wallach. Twenty-two years before that, Evelyn interviewed and hired Ida Wallach. Ida, who retired from Travelers in 1981, wasn't ready to stop working when she turned 65, and she didn't have to. Ida took advantage of the job bank and now shares the receptionist's position in the Data Processing Department with Ruth Eisenberg. Ruth and Ida share their job in half-day segments. They are responsible for answering calls coming in on sixty-two telephones for officers and managers, monitoring and recording all absences and vacations for the Personnel Unit of the Data Processing Department, and greeting visitors. An early riser, Ida works from 7:45 A.M. to noon. She tries to get everything done before turning her desk over to Ruth for the afternoon shift. A true sharer, she doesn't want to leave a mess for her partner. Ida admittedly works for the money, yet she also works "for the fun of it."

Ruth states, "Job sharing is great! It gives two people the opportunity to work. For a retiree, four hours is plenty of time to work. It's enough to keep you happy and to keep you going without being too much work. It's good for us to get out to see what's going on in the world. It gets our minds working and our brains thinking."

Their part-time schedules afford them time to remain active in the job market and also to pursue the interests they never had time for while employed full time.

What is an older worker? According to an article in *Dynamic Years,* even the experts can't decide. U.S. antidiscrimination law uses age 40 as the dividing line between younger and older workers. The Bureau of Labor Statistics thinks in terms of workers 55 or older; "prime" workers, according to the bureau, are those in the 25-to-54-year-old group.

Historically, employers have considered workers to be in the older category when they entered their fifties. By their mid-sixties, of course, workers used to be deemed ready for retirement. Those ideas have changed now that the mandatory retirement age for most workers has been raised to 70.

Moves to prolong the working life recognize that Americans are healthier and living longer. The death rate for people over 65, for example, has dropped 14 percent in the past decade. At 65, average life expectancy is another 15 years; at 75, it is another 10 years. In 1900, average life expectancy at birth was 45 years; today, it is over 70 years.

A recent study by the Work in America Institute, a New

York-based research group, discovered the following traits of workers 50 and older:

They have fewer absences than younger workers.

They have fewer on-the-job accidents.

They are more satisfied with their jobs.

They have less stress on the job than younger workers.

They show lower rates of admission to psychiatric facilities.

Concluded the Work in America Institute: "Within a work group, a balance of ages is desirable to temper the energy and risk-taking of younger people with the maturity, prudence and experience of older people."

In the fall of 1982, *Business Week* conducted a survey of companies rehiring their own retirees. Here are some of their findings:

Lockheed Missiles & Space Co. in Sunnyvale, California, has about sixty retired engineers and scientists working part time.

Honeywell Inc. in Minneapolis, Minnesota, revised its pension plan to let retired employees work on a part-time basis.

State Mutual Life Assurance Company of America in Worcester, Massachusetts, believes so strongly that its former employees do better than outsiders that it routinely approaches them before going to temporary-help agencies to fill posts ranging from secretarial/clerical to management.

Motorola, Inc. in Schaumburg, Illinois, which has rehired retirees for the past three years, keeps a permanent pool of part-time clerical workers and employs specialists on call.

Yale University does not limit the hours retirees may work and, if they work 20 hours a week, returns them to full benefit status. If they work more than 1,000 hours a year, they get pension credit for the additional years of service when they retire for the second time.

Harris Trust & Savings Bank of Chicago, Illinois, has been rehiring its retirees since the 1940s. They report that savings from this program come to $3 to $5 an hour compared with the fees of temporary-help agencies.

Continental Illinois National Bank & Trust Co., also in Chicago, has its own in-house temporary agency. Of these workers, 45 percent are over 65 years old.

Northern Natural Gas Co. has part-time and shared jobs for its older workers.

Among companies considering pension changes to enable retirees to work or to work more hours are Levi Strauss, Grumman Aerospace, Chase Manhattan Bank, and American Telephone & Telegraph.

Underutilization of older Americans in today's work force poses serious problems for them and for our economy. Those critical issues were summarized in a speech given by Morrison H. Beach, chairman of the board of Travelers Insurance Companies of Hartford in March 1981 before the annual conference of the National Council on the Aging.

> . . . The years of the eighties present us with a real challenge to make the economic future of all our older citizens one of dignity and security. What can business do?
>
> First: American business can get to work on one of the most important priorities for older Americans: *jobs for older workers.*
>
> No single achievement by the business community could do more for older citizens and for the country then to open up opportunities for work to the many older people who want to work. It

will require that the business community make a fundamental re-appraisal of its old assumptions about work and retirement.

. . . The national trend is toward longer, healthier life, to-ward more years with more energy, more ability, more need to re-main active.

We know, moreover, that while most older people want to enjoy at least partial retirement, few of them want to be forcibly totally sidelined. A substantial minority of older citizens are will-ing and eager to work. A Harris poll released in 1979 reported that 46 percent of today's retired people would prefer to work, part time or full time. And 51 percent of younger workers—today's workers; tomorrow's retirees—expressed their hope to work in some way after they retire.

We know, finally, that work is good for the older people who choose it, it is good for business—and good for the country.

For older people, the rewards are both economic and psy-chic. Work brings in money to supplement pensions and savings that are increasingly threatened by inflation. And work creates a sense of usefulness, of being involved, active, and needed.

For business, extending work opportunity for older workers is a way to tap a vast reservoir of skill, experience, knowledge and productivity. As the pool of younger workers grows smaller in the future, it is clearly in the self-interest of business to look to our older citizens; to seek ways to continue employment for older workers.

For the country, the benefits of work by older people come not only in supplementing the nation's retirement income pro-grams. Our economic studies for the White House Conference suggest that expanded employment of older workers will boost our whole economy. It could help improve our real Gross National Product by almost four percent over the next 25 years. And this expanded economic growth, in turn, could add about $40 billion in 1980 dollars to Federal, State and local tax revenues in the year 2005. This "fiscal dividend"—created without raising taxes—could then be used to increase the help we give to needy people in America, old and young.

Fortunately, several national trends point in the right direction. Gradually, we seem to be changing our old ideas about work and retirement. The 1978 amendments to the Age Discrimination in Employment Act, for example, wiped out most mandatory retirement ages up to age 70. Compulsory retirement on the basis of age has been almost completely abolished by the Federal government and by several states for their own employees. Social Security laws have been liberalized so that older workers can earn more money without losing benefits.

All this helps, but much more needs to be done. For the fact is this: too few people over 65 who want to work actually *do* work. Last year, fewer than 21 percent of men age 65 to 69 worked even part time—and fewer than 15 percent of women. A majority of these people, as I have said, choose not to work; they want to enjoy complete retirement. But too many older people—healthy, willing and eager—want to work, but can't. They are faced with arbitrary barriers: age discrimination; restrictive government and corporate policies; transportation problems; economic penalties for work effort.

Perhaps the greatest barrier of all facing older citizens seeking jobs is simple lack of choice—for all too often, the only choice the system provides is between full-time work or full-time retirement. It must be our achievement, in the 1980s, to lower these barriers once and for all. We must create real choices for older people. This will require—let us make no mistake—some sweeping changes in public and private policies.

In particular, the business community needs not just to become part of the movement toward work opportunity for older people; business needs to lead that movement. This means changing employment and retirement policies. It means moving to age-neutral hiring policies. It means restructuring jobs to create choices for older workers: the choice, perhaps, of phased retirement and training for second careers. The choice of temporary or part-time work. The choice of job sharing by older workers.

At the company I know best, The Travelers, we have been exploring what we can do to help older Americans. We started in our own corporate household. We eliminated all mandatory retirement ages—even the 70-year limit still permitted by federal law. We did this not just in Connecticut, where it is required by law. We eliminated mandatory retirement ages throughout our company nationwide. Hiring and work at The Travelers will be based on skill, ability, aptitude—not age.

A pre-retirement survey of our employees aged 55 and over suggested several directions for future policy. A large majority of our employees, for example, asked for more and better pre-retirement counseling. And consider this: a whopping 85 percent expressed interest in some form of paid employment after they retire. . . .

. . . Why not make it possible for Travelers retirees to fill temporary jobs in our home office? Such jobs traditionally have been filled by workers from temporary-service agencies. Last year, we hired roughly 65 temporary workers each day from such agencies. Hiring our own retirees to do such jobs appeared to make good sense for everyone. Our retirees, after all, know our company and its systems and the evidence suggests that "Senior Power" is not just a slogan: our older clerical workers outperform younger ones! Establishing our own temporary agency of retirees would save money—making it possible to pay our retirees more than they could earn by working for an outside agency.

This led to another idea: to create job opportunities for retirees who want more permanent, but part-time work. We surveyed all our home office departments and found that more than 300 jobs could be performed on a part-time, *shared* basis by retirees. We made a decision to offer such jobs to our retired workers who want them.

To turn these ideas into reality, we created a Retirees' Job Bank. Through the Job Bank, our retirees can register to fill temporary positions with the company. As permanent, shared job opportunities open up, retirees can find these also through the Job Bank. It gives me great pride, by the way, to add that the Job Bank itself is run to two retirees sharing a full-time position. They are not volunteers; they are paid part-time workers. And one of them is 71 years old. . . .

BIBLIOGRAPHY: OLDER WORKERS

Asbury, Edith Evans. "Some Concerns Try to Keep Older Workers on Job." *New York Times,* 12 April 1981.

Carlson, Elliot. "Going for the Gold," *Dynamic Years,* November–December 1980.

Economic Policy in An Aging Society: A Study of The Future Impact of Public Policy Changes on The Economy and on The Elderly. Final Report of the Technical Committee on an Age-Integrated Society—Implications for the Economy. 1981 White House Conference on Aging, February 15, 1981.

McCarroll, Thomas. "Rehiring Retirees." *New York Times,* 22 November 1981.

Porter, Sylvia. "Firms Expand Job Opportunities for Elderly." New York *Daily News,* 28 June 1981.

Quinn, Laura. "No More '9 to 5 'til 65!' " *The Gray Panther Network,* March–April 1982.

Sommer, Jeff. "For Elderly, Finding Work Is a Hard Job." *Newsday,* Long Island, N.Y.

Stetson, Damon. "More Older Workers Are Seeking Part-Time Jobs." *New York Times,* 24 September 1981.

"When Retirees Go Back on the Payroll," *Business Week,* 22 November 1982.

Yarmon, Morton. "A Return Engagement." *50 Plus,* August 1982.

5

Job Sharing from the Employer's Side

"There's no question that I get 200 percent from my writers. It is a unique interplay of two people, two brains, two different writing styles that work to perfection." That's what Courtney Harmes, director of public affairs at a large hospital, had to say about the team of job sharers she supervised.

"Not only has the productivity of the department increased, but also the quality of the overall public service is rising very quickly. Time is not wasted through simple inactivity or through performance of an it-makes-me-look-busy task," says the supervisor of a shared library assistant position in Wisconsin state government.

Another supervisor of a shared job in the state of Wisconsin notes that "one positive and quite unexpected spin-off we have noticed is that our office has been forced to reexamine and streamline certain processes and abandon or transfer others. It's possible that this might not have occurred if the job sharers hadn't observed how much time they spend on routine paper shuffling. Apparently, one gets a much better view of what constitutes wasted effort from a four-hour-per-day perspective. I just wonder how many wasted steps could be eliminated if we *all* reassessed our jobs."

Employers institute job-sharing programs for a variety of reasons:

Greater flexibility in work scheduling

Retention of valued employees

Reduction of turnover

Wider range of skills in one job title

Recruitment from a broader labor pool

New options for older employees

More energy on the job

Reduction of absenteeism

Continuity of job performance

THE PROS AND CONS

In a management environment, where quality circles; Theories X, Y, or Z; and a whole spectrum of sophisticated techniques are being explored to increase productivity, the factor of enthusiasm should not be overlooked.

Enthusiastic job sharers demonstrate that the quality and quantity of their work increases. Many workers who move from full-time to shared schedules agree that stress and fatigue decrease. Jobs dealing with high-pressure situations benefit from employees who are able to come to their work fresh and relaxed.

Cost-conscious employers observe a positive result at the bottom line because job sharers, at liberty to schedule medical and personal appointments during free time, avoid using sick days or company time for these tasks. Job sharers are more inclined to make time up because they have that extra time to do it. Effective time management cuts the need for extra staff during peak periods. Overtime costs are significantly reduced, and continued job coverage diminishes the need for temporary personnel during vacations and extended illnesses. By responding to the needs of employees who want more free time, job sharing can prevent unnecessary turnover.

In addition to benefiting the organization through increased productivity and reduced costs, job sharing can provide a recruiting edge. Often people with highly desirable skills may not be working because they cannot work full time. These skilled workers may be retirees, heads of families, or the handicapped. Even individuals interested in finding full-time employment are favorably impressed by employers who offer job sharing. The implications of progressive human resource management policies are not lost on today's work force; people are concerned with quality of life.

Naturally, employers question the costs that may be involved in the administration of human resource management and benefits.

Administratively, there will probably be a slight increase in cost, based on the additional paper work.

Training costs are actually reduced in some cases. Sometimes a valued employee remains in a position that otherwise would have required a completely new worker. This incumbent is then able to train the job-sharing partner. It is also worth noting that when one team member leaves, the remaining team member takes over the training process, thus alleviating the need for supervisors to retrain new employees. In any event, the job sharers should overlap during the training period, avoiding the need for repetition.

Supervisors may find that initially they are taking more time to oversee their job-sharing team. Well-designed communication tools for the job-sharing team can lighten this extra load. Also, job-sharing teams have a tendency to supervise one another, catching errors and brainstorming, thereby enhancing their job performance.

As far as employee benefits go, only the statutory benefits would be affected, and those minimally. Social Security costs increase if the base salary for the shared position is above maximum (at present writing, $29,700).

Unemployment insurance varies from state to state. Based on the first $6,000, the unemployment insurance would double on a position paying $12,000 or more a year (at present, approximately $150 per employee). Workers compensation is based on a percentage of payroll, and there would therefore be no difference in the cost.

Concerns about inconvenience are usually grounded in fear of the unknown. If the company establishes time schedules, communication tools, and shared-job responsibilities in advance and communicates these to the relevant people in the organization, they will find that most job-sharing teams slip easily into their slots.

PLANNING

The first shared job your organization provides may result from a single employee's request, or it may be generated by top management. Whatever the reason, good advance planning is essential to the success of the program. Here is a checklist of steps to be taken.

Appoint a Special Coordinator: One person, assisted if necessary by a committee, should be responsible for seeing that all the pieces fall into place. The more directly top management supports and guides the program, the better.

Develop a Timetable: A timetable should be developed outlining the steps to be taken in the job-sharing program and targeting dates for the accomplishment of these tasks. Some steps can be taken concurrently, and these should be indicated on the timetable.

Establish Goals and Objectives: Determine whether job sharing will be offered throughout the organization, to one or more departments, or within a specific job type. Decide whether to offer the program only to current employees and/or company retirees or to recruit from the outside. Specify the number of jobs and job categories. Define goals, and formulate a review process.

Design a Policy Statement: Formally outline what the program means and where it stands in terms of priority.

Review Personnel Policies and Procedures, Relevant Legislation, and Union Contracts: Anticipate stumbling blocks in your present structure, and be prepared with alternatives. For example, if the organization currently utilizes a straight head count system, this will need to be altered so that part-time employees can be prorated.

Open Up Channels of Communication: As soon as policy has been established, everyone concerned should be informed that a job-sharing program is under consideration. It is essential to forestall possible employee apprehensions by clearly communicating the intentions of the program from the very beginning. Stress that job sharing is a *voluntary* work arrangement; that a consensus of opinion among employees, supervisors, management, and bargaining units must be reached before the program is put in place; and that the program has been undertaken as a response to the changing needs of the work force.

Establish Policies and Procedures Governing the Job-Sharing Program: Guidelines must be established regarding eligibility, how benefits will be handled, reversibility of the program (can a shared job be converted back to full time if it doesn't work out? How is this determined? What are the alternatives?), what type of performance review there will be, how an opening will be handled if one sharer leaves, whether an employee can return to full-time work, and what (if any) review process for the entire program has been established.

Hold a Conference with Top and Middle Management: Provide an opportunity for managers and supervisors to voice their concerns. At the same time, the conference will demonstrate top management's support of the program.

Institute a Screening Process with Employees: Interview employees who want to share their jobs. Make sure they understand all the implications of sharing a job, including changes in salary *and* fringe benefits. Evaluate their motivation for sharing; be careful to screen out those who are merely looking to cut back on time spent at a job they already dislike. Job sharing will not alleviate their problems and may create new ones for the organization.

Communicate the Results to the Organization: While the job-sharing program is being developed, it is important to keep employees informed of progress. Co-workers and supervisors play an important role in the success of the job-sharing team. Enlisting their aid and participation makes the program the concern of everyone.

Concurrent with the planning process, you should be examining jobs to be shared and the mechanics involved. There are certain job types that lend themselves especially well to sharing:

Areas where activity levels swing widely from peaks to valleys

Highly pressured jobs with a history of employee burnout

Positions where you have had difficulty recruiting and keeping good people

Jobs that could benefit from a stretched work schedule (e.g., ten rather than eight hours a day)

Situations where boredom saps productivity

Positions requiring a wide variety of skills

THE JOB

If your organization does not have a salary grade structure, you may also want to utilize the Job Analysis Questionnaire (p. 35) as the basis for establishing salary grades. Following each item in the Job Specifications section, there is a number in parentheses. For example:

1. Extent to which work must be performed independently:
   a. Procedures are precise and almost always the same. (1)

This number in the parentheses represents the weight of that specification. Therefore, after the Job Analysis Questionnaire is completed, you should add up the numbers next to the items selected in the Job Specifications section. The job description for manager of administrative services that appears on page 36 would be weighted as follows:

Job Specification	Weight
1. e	(5)
2. c	(3)
3. c	(3)

4. d	(4)
5. h	(8)
6. e	(5)
7. b and d	(3 average)
8. e	(5)
9. c	(3)
10. d	(4)

Thus, the total weight assigned to those job specifications would be 40; because of extended work schedules (i.e., some weekends) and heavy travel requirements, 4 points are added, bringing the total weight to 44.

Following is a listing of salary grades using this weighting system. The determination of salary for each job must also include considerations such as working conditions and physical strain. Moreover, the local market will affect certain salary levels. See the notes at the end of this chapter for sources of information in your area.

SALARY SCALE

Annual Salary (in thousands of dollars)

SALARY GRADE	LOW	MIDDLE	HIGH	WEIGHT
1	10.3	10.9	11.6	13 14 15
2	11.0	11.7	12.2	16 17 18
3	11.7	12.5	13.3	19 20 21
4	10.6	13.3	14.1	22 23 24
5	13.1	14.1	15.0	25 26 27
6	13.8	14.9	15.9	28 29 30
7	15.5	16.6	17.7	31 32 33
8	17.1	18.2	19.5	34 35 36
9	17.5	19.5	21.4	37 38 39
10	20.9	23.1	25.2	40 41 42

11	22.3	24.7	27.1	43 44 45
12	24.3	27.5	30.7	46 47 48
13	28.3	32.3	36.2	49 50 51
14	32.3	37.0	41.7	52 53 54
15	38.3	43.8	54.8	55 56 57
16	42.3	48.5	54.8	58 59 60
17	46.3	53.3	60.3	61 62 63

RECRUITING

Once you have a description for the job to be shared, you can recruit to fill the position. It may be that you already have a request from an employee who wants to share a job. In that case, you need to be sure that the employee has a clear understanding of what is expected and that his or her "egonomics" and economics are compatible with sharing a job. Some basic things to look for are:

Individuals who are basically cooperative

Team candidates who are good communicators

Applicants who are well organized

Applicants who are flexible with regard to both time and task

The Partnership Profile (p. 42) lists all the things you are looking for to fill this job. Use the job description to make up the Profile. Although the job description and inventory list the basic skills needed in the candidates, you have an opportunity to expand the pool of talent in the job. Seek out applicants who are not mirror images of each other, individuals who will create a synergy.

Following is a sample ad for a shared job. To create your own ad, utilize the job description and refer to the list of action verbs on page 67 and the function descriptions that follow it. Your ad should include:

Job title

Four or five most important functions of the job

Any special requirements (e.g., years of experience, education)

Benefits and salary range

The fact that the job is to be *shared*

Explore what you consider the most attractive aspects of the job, and convey them in your ad. Words such as *challenging, stimulating,* and *rewarding* evoke an image of an active, exciting work environment. Try to paint a picture of what the job is like in as few words as possible. Here is a sample ad.

MANAGER
ADMINISTRATIVE SERVICES

Challenging opportunity for experienced administrator to *job share.* Major division of Fortune 500 corporation seeks a seasoned professional to coordinate administrative activities of division, plan and handle all details of Division management meetings, manage Division contributions budget, and supervise Word Processing Center. Associate degree and 3–5 years' experience required. Good starting salary and generous benefits package. Send résumé and covering letter to Box XYZ.

DIVIDING THE JOB

While you are recruiting for your job-sharing team, you can also determine how the job will be shared. It is best to introduce team candidates to each other prior to making a job offer. Be sure that both members of the team understand and agree on the job-sharing design. There are two major considerations: (1) whether the team members will be equal, complementary, or unequal and (2) what (if any) unusual time requirements there are in the job.

_____ Let's use the job description for manager of administrative services to explore how each team type might best do that job. Keep in mind the fact that there are some special time requirements to be considered. There is also a wide range of skills required for the job, from financial planning to policy writing to planning meetings. Following are two models of how the job could be shared. The first model is based on both job sharers having equal status and sharing the job on a collaborative basis.

Model A

The time schedule for this team has been established at two days one week and three days the second week, with a seasonal adjustment for the flurry of annual meetings in January of each year. Both job sharers work full time during that period (about a month), taking their extra days off during the summer months, when things are slower.

Job Duties: Job duties 1 to 4 involve the communication of organization changes and policies and procedures that take place on a routine basis. Each job sharer reviews the policy and procedure and/or organization change that is instituted on his or her day. It is then entered on a master flow chart maintained by both partners. The flow chart indicates when a document comes in, which department or function it relates to (e.g., sales, marketing, manufacturing, research, product design, or accounting), when the divisional draft is due, the department heads who are required to approve the divisional drafts, when they receive the drafts and when they are required to return them, which vice president must

approve the draft, when the president should review the draft, any
further approvals required (e.g., corporate approvals), and when
the final document should be disseminated to the division. Once
completed, it can be removed from the flow chart.

Job duties 5 to 7 involve day-to-day operations and are handled on an "as needed" basis. Folders are maintained for each activity (e.g., requests for telephone equipment, space changes, re-
pairs). Forms are completed for the various requests (as they
would be if one person was handling the job), and the status of
each request is indicated on the form. Each partner reviews the
contents of the folders at the start of his or her day to determine
which activities need to be followed up.

Job duty 8 also uses flow charts in planning for the monthly
management luncheons and the three major management meetings that take place in January. There are ten management luncheons each year, and the job sharers split this task, each being
responsible for all aspects of five luncheons, including speaker
selection, invitations, menu planning, special notes for the president, and so on.

Organization is the key to the success of the annual management meetings. The partners take turns going on site-selection
trips, usually for a week at a time. While one partner is on the
site-selection trip, the other covers part time at the home office,
thus expanding job coverage in a way that was not possible with
one person in the job. These meetings include the annual divisional meeting and West Coast and East Coast sales meetings.
Both partners work on the divisional meeting, and they split the
sales meetings. One partner takes the West Coast one year and the
East Coast the next year. This task has always required strict attention to detail and as such lends itself well to job sharing. The
availability of two people eliminates one person's trying to be in
two places at once because the meetings take place back to back.
For one person, this meant three to four weeks out of the office.

With two people available, backlogs of activities from other aspects of the job are eliminated.

Job duty 9, managing the division contributions budget, is also shared by both partners. This function requires coordination of local contributions budgets from operating units throughout the continental United States, Canada, and Hawaii. Guidelines, established by top management, are sent to each operating manager early in April. They include the prior year's budget, projected earnings for the coming year, and any long-term commitments (e.g., five-year funding of a hospital wing). Each operating manager then prepares a local contributions budget and submits it to headquarters. The job sharers divide the job regionally and review the incoming budgets for their regions to ensure compliance with guidelines. They also monitor their regions to make sure all budgets are submitted on time. Both prepare summaries for their regions and then merge the summaries into one complete divisional contributions budget for the year.

Job duty 10, special projects, may be assigned to an individual job sharer or, more likely, to the team by their supervisor.

The job-sharing team utilizes a variety of communication tools including the red folder, a tape recorder, and a telephone log. They share one full-time secretary.

The second example involves job sharers with unequal backgrounds. One of the partners has a stronger administrative background; therefore, at least at the outset, the second job sharer will be serving an apprenticeship.

Model B

Job Duties: For job duties 1 to 4, the same flow chart described in Model A is used for this job-sharing team. However, Partner A (being the stronger administrator, with experience in this area) reviews each corporate policy and handles rewriting to comply with divisional requirements. Partner B then shepherds the policy and procedures and/or organization through the other steps on the flow chart. During the first year of job sharing, partner A guides partner B through rewriting some documents so that these job duties may be shared more collaboratively in the second year.

Job duties 5 to 7 require a shorter period of training, in that the guidelines for these tasks are fairly standard. Partner B checks with partner A before making any major commitments or ordering equipment.

Because job duty 8 requires more experience, partner B acts as an assistant to partner A during the first year in planning the management luncheons and divisional management meetings. Partner A does all the site-selection travel while training partner B at the local level. Partner B will accompany partner A to at least one of the January meetings.

Job duty 9, managing the division contributions budget, is shared by both partners. However, once the summary for each region is prepared, partner A will review all the budgets and handle the merging into one division contributions budget.

Job duty 10, special projects, is handled on the same basis as in Model A.

Given the training aspect of this job-sharing arrangement, the employees' time was scheduled on a two-and-one-half-days-a-week basis. Partner A works a full day Monday and Thursday and half a day on Wednesday; partner B works a full day Tuesday and Friday and half a day on Wednesday. The partners overlap for a working two-hour lunch on Wednesdays. This team also overlaps during the month of January for the three management meetings.

PERFORMANCE APPRAISAL

Some time ago, the supervisor of a job-sharing team confided that their first performance review was a disaster. Why? Simple. Bill, the supervisor, is a morning person; he is much more aware of what is being accomplished during the earlier part of the day. His job-sharing team was on a half-day schedule. As a result, the morning half of the team got the better review. Fortunately, the afternoon partner spoke up, and the team's schedule was changed so that both partners could be evaluated fairly.

Performance appraisal is one operation that takes more time with a job-sharing team than with a single employee. A two-part evaluation simplifies that process as much as possible: (1) How well was the job accomplished? (2) Was there a marked difference in partner performance?

The following Performance Appraisal Form has been developed for evaluating job sharers. It covers both the job duties (as indicated in the job description) and individual performance.

The performance appraisal interview should be conducted with both members of the team present. Each should be given a copy of your appraisal so that he or she can discuss it with you.

Once the job-sharing program is under way, it is best to schedule the first performance review for six months after the date of hire. Salary reviews should be based on the same merit system used for other employees and at the same intervals. You may also want to have an information review with the supervisor and job sharers after two to three months to iron out any kinks in the program. If you are utilizing a consultant's services, make sure this review is planned for with no consultant present.

Productivity is an elusive commodity. How can you then measure the impact of job sharing on your organization?

The goals and objectives set forth during the planning process will provide one yardstick for measuring results. In addition, you may find that you are attracting a higher caliber of applicant. Your turnover rate for full-time employees may be lower.

Job-sharing programs create a lot of good will among workers, and that spills over into the community in which you operate. An intangible result of your job-sharing program may well be some wider favorable public relations. To what extent your organization is willing to participate in this publicity is your policy decision. Many companies employing job sharers have found themselves overnight stars, with national television, radio, and print coverage touting the farsightedness of their employment programs.

PERFORMANCE APPRAISAL FORM

JOB-SHARING TEAM

TITLE:_____

LOCATION:_____

INCUMBENTS:_____

_____

SUPERVISOR:_____

DATE OF APPRAISAL:_____

Instructions: This appraisal is divided into four parts: Part I
deals with the overall performance of the job and should be based
on the accomplishments achieved. Part II rates the individual job
sharers. Part III rates the job-sharing program within the context
of this particular job. Part IV evaluates training and promotability.

Rating: (A) Excellent, (B) Good, (C) Satisfactory,
         (D) Unsatisfactory

Part I: Indicate in the Performance column whether the job duty
was performed as a team ("A&B"), split ("½A,½B"), or which job sharer
performed the duty ("A"). In the Rating column, rate the performance
of the duty A, B, C, or D.

JOB DUTY	PERFORMANCE	RATING
1. Establish and maintain a Division operating policy and procedure manual.	_____	____
2. Work with Corporate and Division departments in writing and securing approval of policies and procedures.	_____	____
3. Maintain a Division organization manual.	_____	____
4. Establish and monitor internal organization announcements.	_____	____
5. Coordinate Division requirements for administrative services at Head-quarters building.	_____	____
6. Supervise the activities of the Word Processing Center, and establish proce-dures for facilitating the transmission of work to and from the Center.	_____	____
7. Supervise the proper purchase of office equipment, and maintain an inven-tory of all such equipment at the Head-quarters office.	_____	____

8. Plan and handle all administrative details of the Division management luncheons and Division management meetings.   _____   _____

9. Manage the Division contributions budget, which involves the coordination and administration of the activities in this area for all Division locations and the review and making of recommendations on all requests received for funds from Division Headquarters contributions budget.   _____   _____

10. Special projects (list).

_____   _____   _____

_____   _____   _____

Part II: Fill in the names of the job sharers on the lines below "Partner A" and "Partner B." Indicate in each of these columns the rating for the individuals; in the third column, rate the team's overall performance.

CRITERIA	PARTNER A	PARTNER B	OVERALL
	_____	_____	
Establishes goals and communicates well with partner, supervisor and co-workers.	_____	_____	_____
Performs tasks assigned in a timely fashion. Approaches problem solving in a positive manner; explores and recommends alternatives.	_____	_____	_____
Encourages innovation in subordinates.	_____	_____	_____
Considers long-range implications of decisions as well as immediate results.	_____	_____	_____
Demonstrates flexibility in accomplishing task. Understands what needs to be done, and gets it done.	_____	_____	_____
Grasps new assignments, and achieves results. Works well with other departments and outsiders.	_____	_____	_____

<u>Part III</u>: This is an assessment of job sharing within this job context.

1. How has the job been affected by team performance?

    ___ better   ___ same   ___ not as good

1. Does the job-sharing team require additional supervision?

    ___ yes   ___ no   ___ not sure

3. Has anything been added to the job because of the availability of two sets of skills?

    ___ yes   ___ no   ___ not sure

4. Has interaction with other departments or the public been enhanced or hampered?

    ___ enhanced   ___ hampered   ___ not sure

5. Do you recommend that this job be continued on a shared basis?

    ___ yes   ___ no   ___ not sure

6. Why?_____

    _____

    _____

    _____

7. Are there other jobs in your department that would benefit from job sharing?

    ___ yes   ___ no   ___ not sure

8. Which ones? _____

    _____

    _____

<u>Part IV</u>: Training and promotability

1. Further training is recommended for _____ in the area of _____.

2. A promotion can be considered for:

    ___ Partner A   ___ Partner B   ___ the team

3. Both partners require further training before being considered promotable.

    ___ yes   ___ no

BIBLIOGRAPHY FOR EMPLOYERS

Books

Bostwick, Burdette E., III. *Techniques and Strategies for Getting the Job Interview*. New York: John Wiley & Sons, 1981.

Fear, Richard. *The Evaluation Interview*. New York: McGraw-Hill Book Company, 1978.

Gibson, Robert E. *Compensation*. New York: Amacom, 1981.

Griffes, Ernest J.E. *Managing Employee Benefits*. Homewood, Ill.: Dow Jones-Irwin, 1981.

Henderson, Richard I. *Job Descriptions: Critical Documents*. New York: Amacom, 1976.

Kirkpatrick, Donald L. *How to Improve Performance through Appraisal and Coaching*. New York: Amacom, 1982.

Medley, H. Anthony. *Sweaty Palms: The Neglected Art of Being Interviewed*. Belmont, Calif.: Lifetime Learning Publications, 1978.

Stanton, Erwin. *Successful Personnel Recruiting and Selection*. New York: Amacom, 1977.

Wortman, Max, and J. Sporling. *Defining the Manager's Job*. New York: Amacom, 1980.

Articles

Cogger, John W. "Are You A Skilled Interviewer?" *Personnel Journal* (November 1982).

Coll, Albert, Jr. "Flexible Benefits Are a Key to Better Employee Relations." *Personnel Journal* (January 1983).

Foegen, J.H. "Creative Flowering of Employee Benefits." *Business Horizons* (May/June 1982).

Graves, J. Peter. "Let's Put Appraisals Back in Performance Appraisal." *Personnel Journal* (1982).

"Paying Attention to the Employer's Benefit Needs." *Employee Benefit Plan Review* (July 1982).

Robb, Warren D. "Recruitment in the Computer Age." *Personnel Journal* (November 1982).

Winstanley, N.B. "Legal and Ethical Issues in Performance Appraisals." *Harvard Business Review* (November–December 1980).

Appendixes

National Job-Sharing Network

The following is a list of some organizations offering support to job sharers and employers. Included in the list are types of service offered, days and hours of availability, and some sample job titles and organizations where job sharing is utilized. Many organizations charge a fee for their services and request that inquiries be accompanied by a stamped, self-addressed envelope.

ARIZONA

Work/Life Options, 1202 E. Maryland, 2H, Phoenix, AZ 85014 Telephone: (602) 248-9019 Hours: By appointment only

Provides information services to the community about alternative work schedules through workshops and presentations, consultation services to businesses and agencies, documentation of existing jobs utilizing alternative work schedules, and counseling to both job seekers and employers.

113

Shared jobs in the area include:
Preschool director, faculty adviser, receptionist, hairdresser, trainer for city of Tempe, teacher, legal secretary, emergency room and recovery room nurse, minister, public school nurse, social worker.

CALIFORNIA

New Ways to Work, 149 Ninth Street, San Francisco, CA 94103 Telephone: (415) 552-1000 Hours: Monday–Friday, 10:00 A.M.–4:00 P.M.
For potential sharers and job seekers: offers weekly free information meetings on work-time options. Also offers, for small fees, job listings, career resources, seminars, and counseling. For employers: offers consulting, presentations using visual aids, information, and referrals. Provides a newsletter, international information exchange, and publication list.

Flexible Career Associates, P. O. Box 6701, Santa Barbara, CA 93111 (Suite 306, 3704 State Street, Santa Barbara, CA 93105) Telephone: (805) 687-2575 Hours: Daily, 9:00 A.M.–1:00 P.M.
A nonprofit, educational organization providing information on alternative work schedules, particularly permanent part time and job sharing. Reference library, newsletter, workshops, consultation, job listings, speakers, and audiovisual presentations.
Shared jobs in the area include:
Legal secretary; project leader, university research project; chief teller, bank; decorating consultant, paint/wall coverings store; nuclear medical technician, medical clinic; office manager, law firm; staff trainer, university; teacher, public school district; principal, public school district; assistant manager, bank; director of admissions, private school; assistant director, nursery school; field representative, state legislator's office; librarian, college library; laboratory technicians, medical laboratory; director of public relations, nonprofit agency; recreation director, retirement community.

CONNECTICUT

Family and Career Together, Inc. (FACT), Suite 15, 1007 Farmington Avenue, West Hartford, CT 06107 Telephone: (203) 236-4171 Hours: By appointment only

> FACT educates employers (schools, nonprofit organizations and business), individuals, and the general public in the advantages and use of work-time alternatives. FACT provides workshops and seminars for employers with follow-up consultation, general information, and counseling for individuals. Also functions as a resource center.

Shared jobs in the area include:

> Senior personnel representative, nurse practitioner, secretary, data processing specialist, career counselor, social worker, medical secretary, job bank administrator, and teacher.

MAINE

Nancy Hines Viehmann, Consultant for Work Time Options, P. O. Box 78, Cape Porpoise, ME 04014 Telephone: (207) 967-3462 Hours: By appointment only

> Available to conduct workshops or consult with employers interested in learning about or implementing job-sharing or flexible work-time options. Also available to consult with individuals seeking part-time or job-sharing positions.

Shared jobs in the area include:

> Owner/manager, market; program specialist, community programs at university; social worker, center for the blind.

MASSACHUSETTS

Work Options Unlimited, 645 Boylston Street, Boston, MA 02116 Telephone: (617) 247-3600 Hours: By appointment only

> Bimonthly group information sessions for individuals, job-partner registry, employer information, speakers available.

Shared jobs in the area include:

> Coordinator of consumer protection division, suburban city; secre-

tary, chief of medicine at larg ehospital association; professors (husband and wife); legal secretary; secretary/receptionist, president of large university; assistant house master, large university; rehabilitation clinic outpatient nurse, suburban hospital; admissions director, women's college; social worker.

NEW JERSEY

Glassboro State College, Center for Counseling and Career Development, Memorial Hall, Route 322, Glassboro, NJ 08028 Telephone: (609) 445-5282 Hours: Monday–Friday 8:00 A.M.–4:30 P.M.

Offers workshops on career counseling and job-search strategies, adult internship program, and resource for information on alternative work patterns.

Shared jobs in the area include: editor, weekly newspaper; special-needs teacher, public school; staff nurse, visiting nurse association; word processor, high-tech company; accountant, retail store; health educator, prevention center at suburban hospital; advertising account executive, advertising agency.

NEW YORK

Workshare, Inc., 311 East 50th Street, New York, NY 10022, Patricia Lee, President; Telephone: (212) 832-7061 Hours: By appointment only; Nassau County Representative: Carole Levy Enterprises, 15 Laura Way, Westbury, NY 11590 Telephone: (516) 997-4899 Hours: By appointment only

Management consulting firm working with employers and individ-uals to design and develop job-sharing programs. Researches the utility of job sharing in specific departments, locations, or entire organization; provides educational programs for staff and line management; designs job-sharing programs for one position or entire departments; aids in the selection and placement of job sharers. Distributes computerized listing of job sharers and free-lancers seeking job-sharing partners and positions.

Shared jobs in the area include:
Librarian, executive secretary, writer, professor, career counselor, and teacher.

PENNSYLVANIA

Job Partners (of Job Advisory Service), 300 South Craig Street, Pittsburgh, PA 15237 Telephone: (412) 621–0940 Hours: Monday–Friday, 9:00 A.M.–4:00 P.M.; alternate Saturdays, 9:00 A.M.–1:00 P.M.
Job Partners offers employer introductory seminars, program development, staff orientation, and consulting service. For individuals, it offers career counseling, vocational testing, workshops on job hunting and career development, and second-career internship program. Maintains registry for partners and a resource library.
Shared jobs in the area include:
Social worker, nursing home; supervisor of volunteers, nonprofit institute; office manager, secretary, receptionist.

Work Time Options, Inc., 966 Summer Place, Pittsburgh, PA 15243 Telephone: (412) 261–0846 Hours: Monday–Friday, 9:00 A.M.–5:00 P.M.
Educational organization promoting job sharing. Provides information through presentations, workshops, and seminars, counsels prospective sharers and supervisors. Pairing service and management consultation with demonstration models.
Shared jobs in the area include:
Research assistant, office manager, co-directors of placement service.

TEXAS

Austin Women's Center, 1505 West Sixth, Austin, TX 78703 Telephone: (512) 472–3775 Hours: Monday–Friday, 9:00 A.M.–5:00 P.M.
Women's Employment Advocates conducts weekly job-sharing workshops, contacts employers with job-sharing information, maintains a job bank listing of full-time and job-shared positions, and a résumé bank of current job seekers interested in job sharing or full-time employment.

Shared jobs in the area include:
The University of Texas, Air Quality Control Board, Williamson County, Texas Department of Health, University Methodist Church, Austin and Round Rock School Districts, Department of Human Resources, City of Austin, medical, dental, insurance and realtor's offices.

WASHINGTON

Focus, 509 Tenth Avenue East, Seattle, WA 98102 Telephone: (206) 329-7918 Hours: Monday–Friday, 9:00 A.M.–2:30 P.M.
Job-listing clearinghouse, quarterly newsletter and other publications, workshops (job sharing, part time, career fields, job search, interviewing, résumés), seminars and consulting for organizations, library, research projects.
Shared jobs in the area include:
Office manager, personnel technician, director of physical therapy, physician, legal secretary, program coordinator, outreach worker, urban planner, teacher, legislative aide, personnel manager.

Professional Associations

Accounting

National Association of Accountants
1211 Avenue of the Americas
New York, NY 10036
(212) 754-9700

Advertising

American Advertising Federation
1255 Connecticut Avenue, NW
Washington, DC 20036
(202) 659-1800

American Association of Advertising Agencies
666 Third Avenue
New York, NY 10017
(212) 682-2500

Banking

American Bankers Association
1120 Connecticut Avenue, NW
Washington, DC 20036
(202) 467-4000

Independent Bankers Association of America
Suite 202
1625 Massachusetts Avenue, NW
Washington, DC 20036
(202) 332-8980

Broadcasting

National Association of Broadcasters
1771 N Street, NW
Washington, DC 20036
(202) 293-3500

Chemists

American Chemical Society
1155 Sixteenth Street, NW
Washington, DC 20036
(202) 872-4600

Education

National Educational Association (NEA)
1201 Sixteenth Street, NW
Washington, DC 20036
(202) 833-4000

Engineering

National Society of Professional Engineers
2029 K Street, NW
Washington, DC 20006
(202) 463-2300

Information/Data Processing

American Federation of Information Processing Societies, Inc.
210 Summit Avenue
Montvale, NJ 07645

Insurance

Insurance Institute of America
P.O. Box 314
Malvern, PA 19355
(215) 644-2100

Insurance Society of New York
123 William Street
New York, NY 10036
(212) 962-4111

Investment Finance

Association of Investment Brokers
44 Beaver Street
New York, NY 10004
(212) 209-6428

Job Sharing

Flexible Careers, Inc.
Suite 1502
6 East Monroe
Chicago, IL 60603
(312) 236-6028

Flexible Ways to Work
c/o YWCA
1111 S.W. Tenth Avenue
Portland, OR 97205
(503) 241-0537

Focus on Alternate Work Patterns
509 Tenth Avenue East
Seattle, WA 98102
(206) 329-7918

New Ways to Work
149 Ninth Street
San Francisco, CA 94103
(415) 552-1000

National Council for Alternative Work Patterns
Suite 308A
1925 K Street, NW
Washington, DC 20006
(202) 466-4467

Work Options for Women
1358 North Waco Street
Wichita, KS 67203
(316) 264-6604

Workshare, Inc.
311 East Fiftieth Street
New York, NY 10022
(212) 832-7061

Legal

American Bar Association
1155 East Sixtieth Street
Chicago, IL 60637
(312) 947-4000

Library

Special Libraries Association
235 Park Avenue South
New York, NY 10003
(212) 477-9250

Management

Administrative Management Society
Maryland Avenue
Willow Grove, PA 19090
(215) 659-4300

America Management Associations
135 West Fiftieth Street
New York, NY 10020
(212) 586-8100

Marketing

American Marketing Association
Suite 200
250 South Wacker Drive
Chicago, IL 60606
(312) 648-0536

Medical

American Medical Association
535 North Dearborn Street
Chicago, IL 60610
(312) 751-6000

Nursing

American Nurses' Association
2420 Pershing Road
Kansas City, MO 64108
(816) 474-5720

Personnel

American Personnel and Guidance Association
Suite 400
2 Skyline Plaza
5203 Leesburg Pike
Falls Church, VA 22041
(703) 820–4700

American Society for Personnel Administration
30 Park Drive
Berea, OH 44017
(216) 826–4790

Planning

American Planning Association
1313 East Sixtieth Street
Chicago, IL 60637
(312) 947–2560

Psychology

American Psychological Association
1200 Seventeenth Street, NW
Washington, DC 20036
(202) 833–7600

Public Relations

Public Relations Society of America, Inc.
845 Third Avenue
New York, NY 10022
(212) 826–1750

Publishing

Association of American Publishers, Inc.
1 Park Avenue
New York, NY 10016
(212) 689–8920

Purchasing

National Association of Purchasing Management
11 Park Place
New York, NY 10007
(212) 285-2550

Realty

National Association of Realtors
430 North Michigan Avenue
Chicago, IL 60611
(312) 440-8000

Retailing

National Retail Merchants Association
100 West Thirty-first Street
New York, NY 10001
(212) 244-8780

Secretaries

Professional Secretaries International
Suite 6-10
Crown Center
2440 Pershing Road
Kansas City, MO 64108
(816) 474-5755

Training

American Society for Training and Development
600 Maryland Avenue, SW
Washington, DC 20025
(202) 484-2390

Word Processing

American Word Processing Association
P.O. Box 16267
Lansing, MI 48901

REFERENCE BOOKS

Dictionary of Occupational Titles. Washington, D.C.: U.S. Government Printing Office, 1982.

Dun & Bradstreet Million Dollar Directory. Vols. 1, 2, and 3. Parsippany, N.J.: Dun's Marketing Service, 1982.

Encyclopedia of Associations. Vols. 1 and 2. Detroit, Mich.: Gale Research Company, 1983.

The Foundation Directory. 8th ed. New York: Foundation Center, 1981.

Hopke, William E., ed. *Encyclopedia of Careers and Vocational Guidance.* 4th ed. Vol. 1, *Planning Your Careers,* Vol. 2, *Careers and Occupations.* Chicago: Ferguson Publishing Co., 1978.

Literary Market Place. New York: R.R. Bowker Company, 1983.

Occupational Outlook Handbook. Washington, D.C.: U.S. Department of Labor, Bureau of Labor Statistics, 1982-83 Edition.

Standard & Poor's Register of Corporations, Directors, and Executives. New York: Standard & Poor's Corporation, 1982.

Standard Directory of Advertising Agencies. Vols. 1, 2, and 3. Skokie, Ill.: National Register Publishing Co., 1982.

Bibliography

Alvarado, Yolanda. "Lansing Teachers Offered Job Sharing Plan to Avoid Layoffs." *Lansing State Journal* (January 13, 1981).

Angell, Marilyn. "Job Sharing Gives Double Satisfaction." *Scottsdale Daily Progress,* 25 June 1980, p. 15.

Arbose, Jules R. "Putting Nine to Five Up on the Shelf." *International Management* (October 1981).

Askari, Emilia. "Drake Project Helps Promote Job Sharing." *Des Moines Sunday Register,* 1 August 1982.

Azzarone, Stephanie. "More Professionals Working Part-Time." *Money Magazine,* September 1982.

Berkman, Sue. "Half a Job Can Be Better Than One." *Savvy,* March 1981.

Best, Fred. *Exchanging Earnings for Leisure: Findings of an Exploratory National Survey on Work Time Preferences."* Research and Development Monograph, no. 79, Washington, D.C.: U.S. Department of Labor, 1980.

Bingham, Maren S. "Co-Pastors and Congregations Mutually Benefitted." *The Tempe Tribune,* 20 February 1982.

A Booklet of General Information About Job Sharing, New Ways to Work Job Sharing Project, San Francisco, CA, June 1977.

Bravlove, Mary. "Problems of Two-Career Families Start Forcing Businesses to Adapt." *Wall Street Journal,* 15 July 1981.

Brigada, Gerry. "Corporations Welcome New Concept." *Hartford Woman,* December 1981.

127

Carlson, John. "Workers Give Up Pay So Others Keep Jobs." *Des Moines Register.*

Carver, Carol, and Linda J. Crossman. *American Journal of Nursing* (April 1980).

Chamberlin, Patricia A., and Mary D. Jones. "Planning a Shared Schedule Residency." *Journal of Medical Education,* 55 (June 1980).

"Coast Group Finds a Rise in Workers Sharing Jobs." *New York Times,* 26 September 1979.

Connolly, Bill. "Why Not Consider Job Sharing? If It Can Work for TRW Vidar, It Can Work for You." *TRW Vidar,* September 1980.

Coolidge, Joy. "Employer Gets Two Secretaries." *The Arizona Republic,* 17 January 1982.

Dempster, Doug. "One Job, But Two Fill Boss Position." *Sacramento Bee.*

Diggs, J. Frank. "Job Sharing: For Many, A Perfect Answer." *U.S. News and World Report,* 23 August 1982.

Eaker, Kathryn. "Job Sharing: A Growing Alternative to the 40 Hour Grind." *The Sacramento Bee,* 13 July 1980.

Early, Maureen. "Job Sharing—An Idea Whose Time Has Come." *Newsday,* 29 July 1980.

Eskes, Dave. "Share the Work and the Wealth." *Phoenix Gazette,* 27 May 1981.

Filstrup, J. M. "Job/Family Balance: Part-Time Pro." *Vogue,* September 1981.

Frank, Jennifer. "Governor Studying Request to Support Flexible Work Schedules." *Hartford Courant,* 27 January 1982.

Gilman, Robert. "Job Sharing Is Good." *Co-Evolution Quarterly* (Spring 1978).

Grady, Sharon. "One Job, Two Careers." *Working Woman,* March 1981.

"Grants to Encourage Sharing of Jobs." *London Times,* 28 July 1982.

Hager, Philip. "Sisters Hail Job-Sharing, Get 'Best Of Two Worlds.' " *Chicago Sun-Times,* 25 June 1980.

Harper, Keith. "New Cash for Firms if Jobs Are Split." *Manchester Guardian,* 28 July 1982.

"Hiring Shifts to Part-Timers." *New York Times,* 14 December 1981.

Irwin, Victoria. "Job Sharing—A Flexible Solution." *Christian Science Monitor,* 24 January 1980.

Job Sharing: A Manual For Sharing A Job, Alternative Employment Opportunities Study, June 1981.

"Job Sharing: A New Way to Work." *Current Consumer,* October 1981.

"Job-Sharing—Another Way to Work." *Worklife,* 3, no. 5 (May 1978).

" 'Job Sharing' Becoming Popular as a Working Arrangement." *Chicago Tribune,* 18 September 1979.

"Job Sharing Catches On." *Business Week,* 25 October 1976.

"Job Sharing—Wave of Future Working in the 80's." *Area Agencies on Aging Association,* 2, no. 4.

Kleiman, Carol. "Two Share Job as Governor's Aide." *Chicago Tribune,* 27 December 1981.

Lane, Millicent. "Job-Sharers Blaze Path Here." *Lansing State Journal* (12 May 1981).

Lee, Patricia. "Job Sharing: Teams of Two Tackle the Workplace." *The NOW York Woman,* October 1981.

Lindorff, Dave. "Advice to the Job-Lorn: Job-Sharing." *Soho News,* 8 October 1980.

Linscott, Judy. "Getting Ahead." *Daily News,* 18 November 1980.

Lloyd, John. "Scheme to Cut Jobless." *Financial Times,* 28 July 1982.

Lublin, Joann S. "Mutual Aid: Firms and Job Seekers Find Benefits in Part-Time Work." *Wall Street Journal,* 4 October 1978.

MacDonald, Charlotte. "Job-Sharing: Part-Time Work, Full-Time Potential." *Woman's Day,* 28 June 1977.

McGarry, Donna Dewitt. "Job-Sharing—Job Satisfaction." *Business Journal in Minnesota.*

Markels, Marcia, and Barney Olmsted. *Working Less But Enjoying It More,* San Francisco: New Ways to Work, 1978.

Meier, Gretl S. *Job Sharing: A New Pattern for Quality of Work and Life.* Upjohn Institute, 1978.

Miller, Darla. "Divided Jobs May Conquer the Workplace." *San Jose Mercury,* 1 July 1981.

Moorman, Barbara, Suzanne Smith, and Susie Ruggels. *Job Sharing in the Schools*. San Francisco: New Ways to Work, 1980.

————. *Job Sharing in the Schools: Guides to Policies and Contracts*. San Francisco: New Ways to Work, 1980.

Olmsted, Barney. "Job Sharing—A New Way to Work." *Personnel Journal* (February 1977).

Pechman, Susan. "Why Not Negotiate a Shared Job?" *Woman's Day*, 28 April 1981.

Piasecki, Cris. *Job Sharing at T.R.W. Vidar—It's Working*. T.R.W. Vidar, Sunnyvale, California, July 1980.

Pilate, Cheryl. "Job Sharing: A Boon to All Parties." *The Wichita Eagle*, 2 June 1980.

Post, Susan W. "How To (Job Share)." *NCAWP Newsletter*.

"Project Ideas For Executive Members." *Alert*, The Research Institute of America, New York.

Project J.O.I.N.: Final Report and Manual for Replication. State of Wisconsin, Division of Human Resource Services, Department of Employment Relations, Federal Manpower Programs Section, June 1979.

Purnick, Joyce. "Koch to Modify 9–5 Jobs to Suit Needs of Employees. *New York Times*, October 1980.

Riegelhaupt, Barbara. "Half a Job for Two Is Better Than One." *Valley News*, 25 June 1980.

Rosley, Joan. "Job Sharing Offers Innovative Opportunities." *Tempe Daily News*, 28 January 1982.

Ross, Cissy. "Group Seeks Greater Job Efficiency, Variable Work Schedules Urged." *Santa Barbara News-Press*, 1 November 1981.

Rossi, Paulette. "Flexible Ways to Work: A Viable Nine-to-Five Alternative." *Portland Magazine*, December 1981.

Roszsnyai, Jean. "Job-Sharing for Chemists—Can't Work?" *American Chemist Society* (6 June 1978).

Schorer, Jane. "Why Are These Women Smiling?" *Des Moines Register*, 20 August 1982.

Scragg, Dana. "Job Sharing: A Working Alternative for Employers and Employees." *Austin*, January 1982.

"Secretarial Shortage: The Job-Sharing Solution." *Personnel Advisory Bulletin,* Bureau of Business Practice, 1980.

Shackelford, Arn. "Job Sharing: The Best of Both Worlds." *Grand Rapids Press,* 28 June 1981.

"Sharing a Job to Spread Employment." *International Management* (November 1981).

Sheehan, Hal. "Over Mechanicville Way." *Schenectady Gazette,* 13 December 1980.

Taylor, Marianne. "Job Sharing—Splitting the Workload Can Be Surprisingly Simple." *Chicago Tribune,* 12 April 1981.

"Two Stanford Nurses Develop Unusual Approach to Job." *Campus Report* (29 October 1980).

Unger, Mike. "When a Single Job Is Shared by Two." *Newsday,* 22 September 1981.

Weil, Debbie. "Work Part Time; Live Full Time." *Atlanta Constitution,* 3 November 1981.

Winfrey, Carey. "Job Sharing—A Working Alternative." *New York Times,* 8 January 1980.

Wolman, Jonathan. "Workplace 2000: The Demise of the 9–5 Work Week." *San Francisco Examiner,* 20 August 1978.

"Worksharing." *Showcase,* 2 (January 1981).

Zettenberg, Carol Gillis. *A Look at Job Teaming.* Levittown, Pa.: Project Job Team, 1978.

Index

133